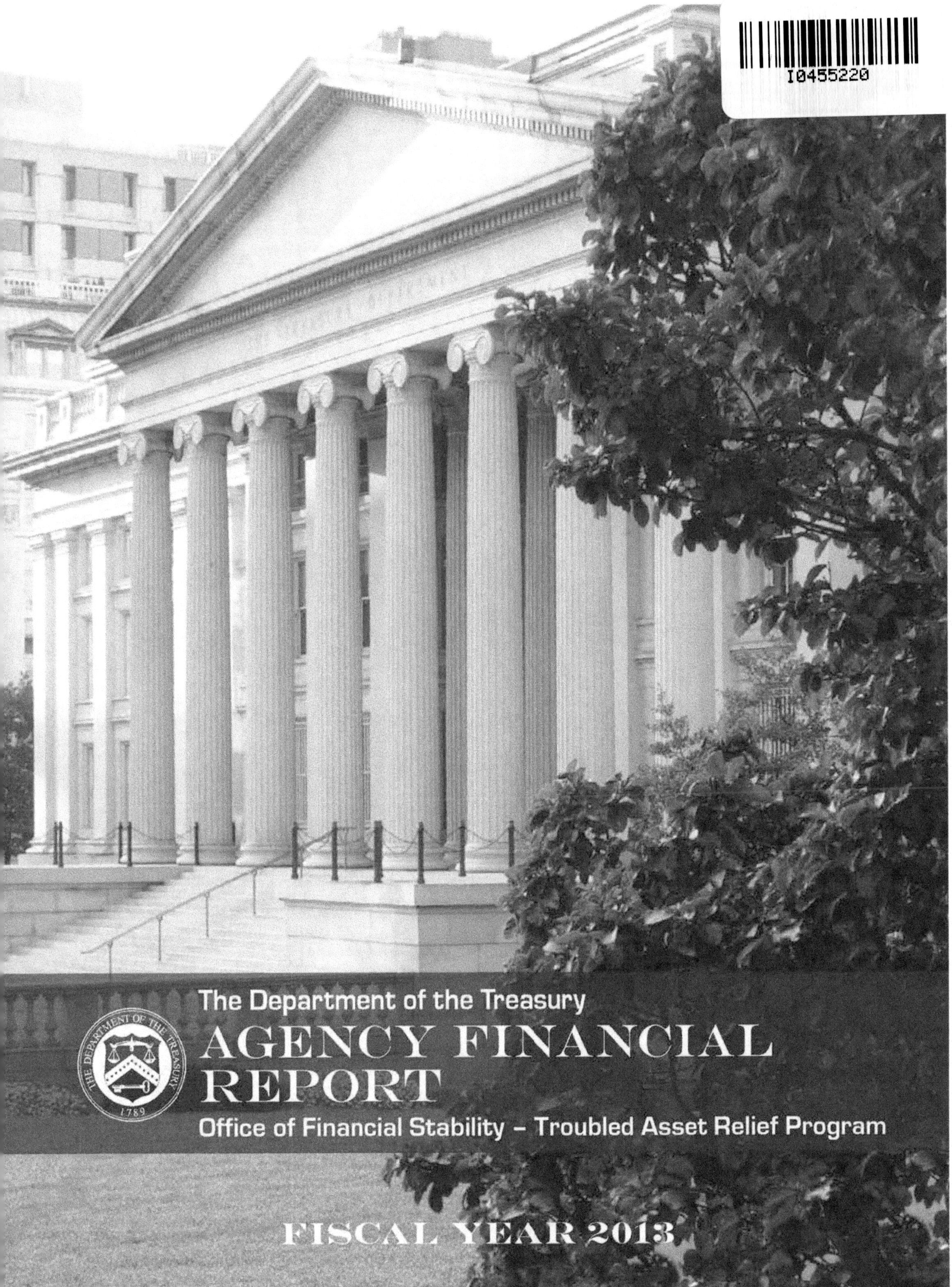

The Department of the Treasury

AGENCY FINANCIAL REPORT

Office of Financial Stability – Troubled Asset Relief Program

FISCAL YEAR 2013

GAO U.S. GOVERNMENT ACCOUNTABILITY OFFICE

441 G St. N.W.
Washington, DC 20548

December 11, 2013

Congressional Committees

Financial Audit: Office of Financial Stability (Troubled Asset Relief Program) Fiscal Years 2013 and 2012 Financial Statements

This report transmits the GAO auditor's report on the results of our audit of the fiscal years 2013 and 2012 financial statements of the Office of Financial Stability (Troubled Asset Relief Program), which is incorporated in the enclosed *Office of Financial Stability (Troubled Asset Relief Program) Agency Financial Report for Fiscal Year 2013*.

As discussed more fully in the auditor's report that begins on page 34 of the enclosed agency financial report, we found

- the Office of Financial Stability's (OFS) financial statements for the Troubled Asset Relief Program (TARP) as of and for the fiscal years ended September 30, 2013, and 2012, are presented fairly, in all material respects, in accordance with U.S. generally accepted accounting principles;
- OFS maintained, in all material respects, effective internal control over financial reporting for TARP as of September 30, 2013; and
- no reportable noncompliance for fiscal year 2013 with provisions of applicable laws, regulations, contracts, and grant agreements we tested.

The Emergency Economic Stabilization Act of 2008 (EESA)[1] that authorized TARP on October 3, 2008, requires that TARP, which is implemented by OFS,[2] annually prepare and submit to Congress and the public audited fiscal year financial statements that are prepared in accordance with U.S. generally accepted accounting principles.[3] EESA further requires that GAO audit TARP's financial statements annually.[4] We are also required under EESA to report at least every 60 days on the findings resulting from our oversight of the actions taken under TARP.[5] This report responds to both of these requirements.

We are sending copies of this report to the Secretary of the Treasury, the Assistant Secretary for Financial Stability, the Financial Stability Oversight Board, the Special Inspector General for TARP, the Director of the Office of Management and Budget, interested congressional committees and members, and other interested parties. In addition, the report is available at no charge on the GAO website at http://www.gao.gov.

---

[1] Pub. L. No. 110-343, div. A, 122 Stat 3765 (Oct. 3, 2008), *classified in part, as amended, at* 12 U.S.C. §§ 5201-5261.

[2] Section 101 of EESA, 12 U.S.C. § 5211, established OFS within the Department of the Treasury to implement TARP.

[3] EESA § 116(b), 12 U.S.C. § 5226(b).

[4] EESA § 116(b), 12 U.S.C. § 5226(b).

[5] EESA § 116(a)(3), 12 U.S.C. § 5226(a)(3).

If you or your staffs have questions about this report, please contact me at (202) 512-3406 or engelg@gao.gov. Contact points for our Offices of Congressional Relations and Public Affairs may be found on the last page of this report.

Gary T. Engel
Director
Financial Management and Assurance

Enclosure

List of Congressional Committees

The Honorable Barbara A. Mikulski
Chairwoman
The Honorable Richard C. Shelby
Vice Chairman
Committee on Appropriations
United States Senate

The Honorable Tim Johnson
Chairman
The Honorable Mike Crapo
Ranking Member
Committee on Banking, Housing, and Urban Affairs
United States Senate

The Honorable Patty Murray
Chairman
The Honorable Jeff Sessions
Ranking Member
Committee on the Budget
United States Senate

The Honorable Max Baucus
Chairman
The Honorable Orrin G. Hatch
Ranking Member
Committee on Finance
United States Senate

The Honorable Harold Rogers
Chairman
The Honorable Nita M. Lowey
Ranking Member
Committee on Appropriations
House of Representatives

The Honorable Paul Ryan
Chairman
The Honorable Chris Van Hollen
Ranking Member
Committee on the Budget
House of Representatives

The Honorable Jeb Hensarling
Chairman
The Honorable Maxine Waters
Ranking Member
Committee on Financial Services
House of Representatives

The Honorable David Camp
Chairman
The Honorable Sander Levin
Ranking Member
Committee on Ways and Means
House of Representatives

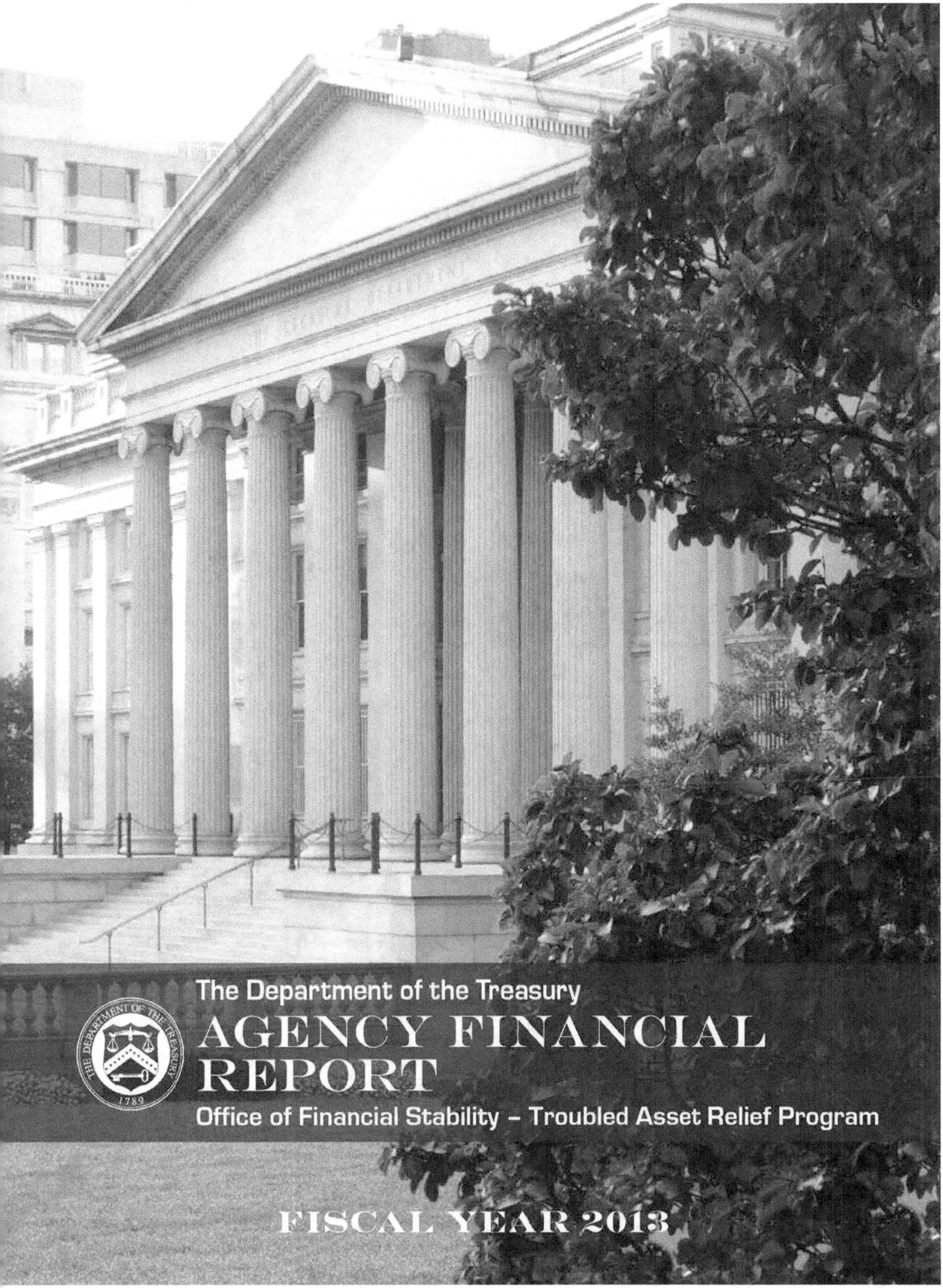

The Department of the Treasury

AGENCY FINANCIAL REPORT

Office of Financial Stability – Troubled Asset Relief Program

FISCAL YEAR 2013

2012 CERTIFICATE OF EXCELLENCE

THE DEPARTMENT OF THE TREASURY
AGENCY FINANCIAL REPORT
Office of Financial Stability – Troubled Asset Relief Program

Fiscal Year 2012

AGA.

CERTIFICATE OF EXCELLENCE IN ACCOUNTABILITY REPORTING

Presented to the

U.S. Department of the Treasury, Office of Financial Stability

In recognition of your outstanding efforts
in preparing the Agency Financial Report and
Summary of Performance and Financial Information
for the fiscal year ended September 30, 2012.

*A Certificate of Excellence in Accountability Reporting is presented
by AGA to federal government agencies whose Agency
Financial Reports achieve the highest standards demonstrating
accountability and communicating results.*

Robert F. Dacey, CGFM, CPA
Chair, Certificate of Excellence
in Accountability Reporting Board

Relmond P. Van Daniker, DBA, CPA
Executive Director, AGA

Table of Contents

MESSAGE FROM THE ASSISTANT SECRETARY FOR FINANCIAL STABILITY

December 5, 2013

I am pleased to present the Office of Financial Stability's (OFS) Agency Financial Report for the Fiscal Year 2013. This report describes our financial and performance results for the fifth year of the Troubled Asset Relief Program (TARP). Within this report you will find the comparative fiscal years 2013 and 2012 financial statements for TARP, the Government Accountability Office's (GAO) audit opinion on these financial statements, a separate opinion from the GAO on OFS's internal control over financial reporting, and the results of the GAO's tests of OFS's compliance with selected provisions of laws, regulations, contracts, and grant agreements applicable to OFS.

The Emergency Economic Stabilization Act (EESA) of 2008 established OFS within the Office of Domestic Finance at the Department of the Treasury to implement TARP. With the nation in the midst of the worst financial crisis since the Great Depression, TARP was created to "restore the liquidity and stability of the financial system." It was an extraordinary response to an extraordinary crisis.

Today, it is generally agreed that as a result of the forceful and coordinated response by the federal government through TARP and many other emergency programs, we helped avert what could have been a devastating collapse of our financial system. Although we are still repairing the damage from the crisis and many families still face challenges on a daily basis, the financial system is much more stable and our economy is growing, albeit not as fast as we would like. Credit is more available than would otherwise be the case for families, businesses, and local governments, banks are better capitalized, and we are implementing reforms to address the underlying causes of the crisis.

In addition, OFS has made significant progress towards winding down TARP investments. As of September 30, 2013, OFS had collected 96.2 percent of the $421.6 billion in program funds that were disbursed under TARP, as well as an additional $17.5 billion from Treasury's equity in AIG. Here is where we stand concerning the four categories of TARP investment programs:

- **Banking Programs.** OFS has collected a total of $273.4 billion (including $6.4 billion collected in fiscal year 2013) for all TARP bank support programs through repayments, sales, dividends, interest, and other income compared to $245.5 billion invested. As of September 30, 2013, $3.6 billion in banking program investments remained outstanding, primarily in community banks, and OFS is continuing to wind-down these investments through repurchases by banks, asset sales, and restructurings.

- **Credit Market Programs**. OFS has substantially completed the wind-down of all of the TARP credit market programs, including investments made under the Public-Private Investment Program (PPIP), Term Asset-Backed Securities Loan Facility (TALF) program, and SBA 7(a) Securities Purchase Program. As of the end of fiscal year 2013, OFS collected $23.5 billion as compared to $19.1 billion of disbursements under these programs.

- **Auto Industry Financing Program**. As of September, 30 2013, OFS has collected $53.3 billion through sales, repayments, dividends, interest, and other income, compared to the $79.7 billion in funds that were disbursed under the Automotive Industry Financing Program (AIFP). Chrysler exited the program in July 2011 and the wind-down of General Motors (GM) is anticipated to be completed by December 31, 2013. In November 2013, OFS received additional repayment of $5.9 billion from Ally Financial Inc. (Ally) under an agreement announced in August. As a result, OFS has recovered over 70% of the investment in Ally Financial Inc. (Ally) through repayments, dividends, and proceeds in excess of costs. OFS is actively seeking to wind-down the remaining investment in Ally.

- **American International Group**. In fiscal year 2013, OFS exited all remaining holdings in American International Group, Inc. (AIG). During the financial crisis, the peak amount of assistance provided by OFS and the Federal Reserve to prevent the collapse of AIG totaled $182.3 billion, a part of which was later cancelled. As a result of the combined efforts of AIG, Treasury, and the Federal Reserve, $22.7 billion in excess of the total of funds disbursed to AIG has been recovered through sales and other income. Of the $67.8 billion total disbursed to AIG by OFS, TARP's cumulative net proceeds from repayments, sales, dividends, interest, and other income related to AIG assets totaled $55.3 billion. As Treasury's non-TARP AIG shares generated proceeds in excess of cost of $17.5 billion, total net proceeds in excess of cost were $5.0 billion for Treasury as a whole.

While OFS carefully winds down the investment programs under TARP, we are continuing to implement the TARP Housing Programs to help millions of struggling homeowners avoid foreclosure, primarily through mortgage modifications and other forms of assistance. These programs (includes government sponsored enterprise (GSE) and non-GSE) have also set new mortgage modification and consumer protection standards which have helped to transform the mortgage servicing industry and thereby help millions more families. On May 30, 2013, the Obama Administration extended the application deadline for the Making Home Affordable Program through December 2015 in order to provide struggling homeowners additional time to access sustainable mortgage relief.

The financial and performance data contained in this report are reliable and complete. For the fifth consecutive year, OFS has earned unmodified opinions on its financial statements and its internal control over financial reporting from the GAO. In 2013, OFS was also awarded its fourth consecutive Certificate of Excellence in Accountability Reporting by the Association of Government Accountants.

This marks my last financial report, as I will step down as Assistant Secretary for Financial Stability this month. Since the spring of 2009, it has been an honor and privilege to serve my country by helping to respond to this terrible financial crisis. TARP did what it was supposed to do—it helped to stabilize our financial system and it did so faster, better and cheaper than most people expected. We should never forget the true costs of the financial crisis in human suffering and economic damage—the jobs lost, the foreclosed homes, the college educations that could not be financed, and the retirements that must be postponed. But without the government's forceful response, the damage would have been far worse and the costs to repair that damage would have been far higher.

Sincerely,

Timothy G. Massad
Assistant Secretary for Financial Stability

EXECUTIVE SUMMARY

The U.S. Department of Treasury's (Treasury), Office of Financial Stability (OFS) presents to the reader the fiscal year 2013 Agency Financial Report (AFR) for the Troubled Asset Relief Program (TARP). The enclosed Management's Discussion and Analysis (MD&A) is required supplementary information to the financial statements and provides a high level overview of OFS, which is the office within the Treasury that was established to implement TARP, pursuant to the Emergency Economic Stabilization Act of 2008 (EESA).

Five years ago, the U.S. financial system faced challenges on a scale not seen since the Great Depression. The banks and financial markets that American families and businesses rely on to meet their everyday financing needs were on the brink of failure. By October 2008, major financial institutions were threatened and many of them tried to shore up their balance sheets by shedding risky assets and hoarding cash. People were rapidly losing trust and confidence in the stability of America's financial system and the capacity of the government to contain the damage. Without immediate and forceful action by the federal government, the U.S. economy faced the risk of falling into a second Great Depression.

It was out of these extraordinary circumstances in the fall of 2008 that TARP was created as a central part of a series of emergency measures by the federal government. Collectively, TARP and the federal government's other emergency programs helped to prevent the collapse of our financial system. As a result of the careful design, implementation, and coordination of these programs, the federal government was able to limit the broader financial and economic damage caused by the crisis. Although we are still recovering, these measures were critical to

restarting economic growth, and in restoring access to capital and credit.

Since late 2010 when OFS's authority to make new commitments under TARP expired, OFS has focused on carefully winding down TARP's investment programs, recovering the OFS's outstanding investments, and continuing to implement the various housing programs under TARP to help struggling homeowners avoid foreclosure. While the total disbursed for TARP programs was $421.6 billion, OFS has collected $405.5 billion (or $423.0 billion if including the $17.5 billion in proceeds from the additional Treasury AIG shares discussed on page 14) through repayments, sales, dividends, interest, and other income. As of September 30, 2013, only $23.5 billion in investments remain outstanding.

The MD&A highlights the establishment of OFS, its background, mission, organizational structure, and programs. OFS administers programs that fall into two major categories: Investment and Housing. In total, OFS has responsibility for 12 individual programs. Most of these programs have either been closed or are in the process of winding down.

Each year, OFS reports on our Operational Goals, which were developed by management to achieve our strategic goal of ensuring the overall stability and liquidity of the financial system, preventing avoidable foreclosures, and by preserving homeownership. The first operational goal for OFS is to complete the wind-down of the TARP investment programs. OFS is continuing to implement the three-pronged exit strategy, announced in May 2012, for the Capital Purchase Program (CPP). That strategy includes waiting for those banks that are able to repay in full in the near future to do so, restructuring OFS's investments in limited cases, and selling investments through auctions in cases where the bank is not expected to repay in the near future. As of September 30, 2013, both the Targeted Investment Program (TIP) and the Asset Guarantee Program (AGP) were closed and have generated positive returns on behalf of taxpayers.

As of September 30, 2013, OFS has substantially completed the wind-down of the three TARP credit market programs which resulted in a positive return on behalf of taxpayers. OFS has recovered all debt and equity investments made in the Public-Private Investment Program (PPIP). OFS's loan commitment made through the Term Asset-Backed Securities Loan Facility (TALF) was fully repaid or extinguished during fiscal year 2013. The Small Business Administration 7(a) Securities Purchase Program (SBA 7(a)) was successfully closed during fiscal year 2012 with the processing of the fifth and final disposition of securities.

OFS continues to wind-down the Automotive Industry Financing Program (AIFP) with the sale of 399 million shares of GM common stock during fiscal year 2013. These sales were conducted according to the plan announced in December 2012 to sell OFS's remaining shares in GM within the next 12-15 months, subject to market conditions. In November 2013, per an August 2013 agreement, OFS collected a total of $5.9 billion from Ally, as it repurchased all of its MCP stock from OFS and paid the agency to eliminate certain rights under the original agreement. OFS is actively seeking to wind-down the remaining investment.

OFS exited its remaining holdings in the American International Group, Inc. (AIG) Investment Program in December 2012 and sold remaining warrants in March 2013. As of September 30, 2013, OFS does not hold any residual interest in AIG.

OFS's second operational goal is to continue helping struggling homeowners avoid foreclosure. The Making Home Affordable Program (MHA) is helping homeowners and assisting in stabilizing the housing market. On May 30, 2013, the Administration extended the application deadline for MHA programs through December 31, 2015, to provide struggling homeowners additional time to access sustainable mortgage relief, and to align the end date with other key assistance programs. The largest program within MHA is the Home Affordable Modification Program (HAMP). Under this program more than 1.4 million homeowners have had their mortgages modified permanently. HAMP has also set new standards and changed practices throughout the mortgage servicing industry in fundamental ways. In addition, the Hardest Hit Fund provides funding to 18 states and the District of Columbia to provide assistance to struggling homeowners through locally-tailored programs. All 19 programs are fully operational and have created extensive infrastructures to operate these programs, including selecting and training networks of housing counselors to assist with applications, creating portals to aid homeowners in applying for assistance, and hiring underwriters and other staff to review and approve applications.

The third operational goal of OFS is to minimize the cost of the TARP programs to the taxpayer. OFS manages TARP investments to minimize costs to taxpayers by carefully managing the timely exit of these investments to reduce taxpayers' exposure, returning TARP funds to reduce the federal debt, and continuing to replace government assistance with private capital in the financial system. OFS has taken a number of steps during fiscal years 2012 and 2013 to dispose of its outstanding investments in a manner that balances the need to exit these investments as quickly as practicable with maximizing returns on behalf of taxpayers. OFS also takes steps to ensure that TARP recipients comply with any TARP-related statutory or contractual obligations such as executive compensation requirements and restrictions on dividend payments.

OFS's final goal is to continue to operate with the highest standards of transparency, accountability, and integrity. OFS posts a variety of reports online that provide the reader with regular and comprehensive information about how TARP funds are being spent, who has received them and on what terms, and how much has been collected to date. As part of this effort, in June 2013, OFS enhanced and expanded the existing TARP Tracker on its website to enable users to view the flow of funds for a specific time period or over the lifetime of a TARP program. OFS also publishes the audited annual report. In addition, OFS continues to maintain productive working relationships with three oversight bodies charged with auditing and reviewing the TARP activities.

In addition to discussing program performance, the MD&A also addresses OFS's financial performance in the *Fiscal Year 2013 and 2012 Financial Summary and Cumulative Net Income* section. OFS provides an overview of its financial data and explains its fiscal year 2013 net income from operations and related loans, equity investments and other credit programs.

Finally, the *Systems, Controls, and Legal Compliance* section of the MD&A provides a discussion of the actions OFS has taken to address its management control responsibilities. This section includes OFS's assurance related to the Federal Manager's Financial Integrity Act, the determination of its compliance with both the Federal Financial Management Improvement Act and the Improper Payment Elimination and Recovery Act.

PART 1: Management's Discussion and Analysis
Background, OFS Organization Structure and Programs

Background

In response to the worst financial crisis since the Great Depression, the Troubled Asset Relief Program (TARP) was created pursuant to the Emergency Economic Stabilization Act (EESA) on October 3, 2008. To carry out the authorities given to the Secretary of the Treasury to implement TARP, the U.S. Department of the Treasury (Treasury) established the Office of Financial Stability (OFS) within the Office of Domestic Finance. EESA authorized the Secretary of the Treasury to establish TARP to "purchase, and to make and fund commitments to purchase, troubled assets from any financial institution, on terms and conditions as are determined by the Secretary" to restore the liquidity and stability of the financial system. The terms "troubled assets" and "financial institution" are defined within EESA, which can be found at: http://www.gpo.gov/fdsys/pkg/BILLS-110hr1424enr/pdf/BILLS-110hr1424enr.pdf. In addition, Section 109 of EESA provides authority to assist homeowners.

The Dodd-Frank Wall Street Reform and Consumer Protection Act (the Dodd-Frank Act), signed into law in July 2010, reduced total TARP purchase authority from $700 billion to a cumulative $475 billion. OFS's authority to make new commitments under TARP expired on October 3, 2010. OFS is carefully managing the disposition of TARP financial assets to recover OFS's outstanding investments while continuing to implement initiatives to help struggling homeowners avoid foreclosure.

OFS Organization Structure

OFS is headed by the Assistant Secretary for Financial Stability. Reporting to the Assistant Secretary are six major organizations the: Office of the Chief Investment Officer, Office of

Finance and Operations, Office of the Chief of Home Ownership Preservation, Office of Financial Agents, Office of the Chief Reporting Officer, and Office of the Chief Compliance Officer. A Chief Counsel's Office also reports to the Assistant Secretary and to the Office of the General Counsel in the Department of the Treasury.

OFS is not envisioned as a permanent organization, so to the maximum extent possible when economically efficient and appropriate, OFS utilizes private sector expertise in support of the execution and liquidation of TARP programs. These firms assist in the areas of custodial services, accounting and internal controls, administrative support, legal advisory, financial advisory, and information technology.

The OFS organization chart follows:

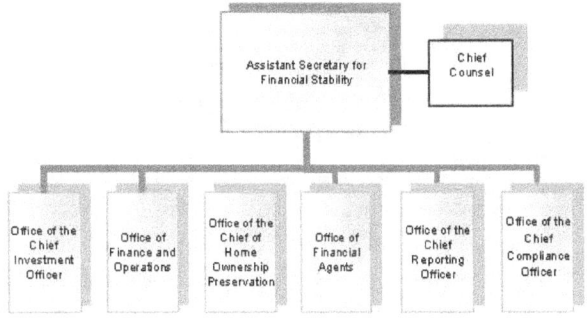

OFS Programs

Bank Support Programs (CPP, TIP, AGP, CDCI, CAP, SCAP)

By late September 2008, several major financial institutions had already failed. Many others were at risk of failure and people were rapidly losing confidence in the nation's financial system as a whole. Therefore beginning in early October 2008, OFS launched five programs to help stabilize the nation's banking institutions. A total of $245.5 billion was invested through TARP bank support programs.

Capital Purchase Program

The Capital Purchase Program (CPP) was launched in October 2008 to help stabilize the financial system by providing capital to viable financial institutions of all sizes throughout the nation. Without a viable banking system, lending to businesses and consumers could have frozen and the financial crisis might have spiraled further out of control. Based on market indicators at the time, it was clear that financial institutions needed additional capital to absorb losses and restart the flow of credit to businesses and consumers to avert a potential collapse of the system.

With the additional capital, CPP participants were better equipped to undertake new lending and continue to provide other services to consumers and businesses, even while absorbing write-downs and charge-offs on loans that were not performing. OFS received preferred stock or debt securities in exchange for the CPP investments. Most financial institutions participating in the CPP pay OFS a five percent dividend on preferred shares for the first five years and a nine percent rate thereafter. In addition, OFS received warrants to purchase common shares or other securities from the banks at the time of the CPP investment. The purpose of the additional securities was to enable OFS to receive additional returns on its investments as banks recover.

OFS has focused on winding down the CPP according to the exit strategy announced on May 3, 2012. That strategy includes a combination of repayments in the case of banks which are expected to repay in the near future, selling OFS's positions in banks that are unlikely to repay in the near-term through auctions, and restructuring some investments, typically in connection with a merger or other plan of the bank to infuse capital, in a way that maximizes timely OFS collections and helps avoid bank failures.

Targeted Investment Program

OFS established the Targeted Investment Program (TIP) in December 2008. The program gave OFS the necessary flexibility to provide funding to financial institutions that were critical to the functioning of the U.S. financial system to prevent a loss of confidence in these critical institutions. This could have resulted in substantial disruption to financial markets, threatened the financial strength of similarly situated financial institutions and undermined the overall economy.

OFS invested a total of $40.0 billion in two institutions – Bank of America (BofA) and Citigroup – under the TIP. These investments were made in addition to those that the banks received under the CPP. Similar to the CPP, OFS invested in preferred stock and received warrants to purchase common stock in each institution.

The TIP investments provided for annual dividends of eight percent, which was higher than the initial CPP rate. The program also imposed greater reporting requirements and more onerous terms on the companies than under the CPP terms, including restricting common stock dividends to $0.01 per share per quarter, restrictions on executive compensation, restrictions on corporate expenses, and other measures.

Asset Guarantee Program

Under the Asset Guarantee Program (AGP), TARP commitments were used to support two institutions – BofA and Citigroup. They were selected because of the large number of illiquid assets that both of them held at the time of the financial crisis and the severe impact that their failure would have had on the broader economy. In January 2009, OFS, the Federal Reserve, and the Federal Deposit Insurance Corporation (FDIC) agreed in principle to share potential losses on a $118 billion pool of financial instruments owned by BofA. However, in May 2009, before the transaction was finalized, BofA decided to terminate negotiations, and in September 2009, the government and BofA entered into an agreement under which the bank agreed to pay a termination fee of $425 million to the government, $276 million of which went to OFS. In January 2009, OFS, the Federal Reserve, and the FDIC similarly agreed to share potential losses on a $301 billion pool of Citigroup's covered assets. The arrangement was finalized and, as a premium for the guarantee, OFS and the FDIC received $7.0 billion of Citigroup preferred stock of which $2.2 billion was OFS's portion. OFS also received warrants to purchase 66.5 million shares of common stock.

Community Development Capital Initiative

OFS created the Community Development Capital Initiative (CDCI) on February 3, 2010, to help viable certified Community Development Financial Institutions (CDFIs) and the communities they serve cope with effects of the financial crisis. It was put in place to help keep day-to-day financing available to families and businesses in hard-hit communities that are underserved by traditional banks.

Since many CDFIs don't have the same access to capital markets as larger banks, the CDCI was designed with more generous terms than the CPP. Under this program, CDFI banks, thrifts, and credit unions received investments aggregating $570 million in capital with an initial dividend or interest rate of two percent, compared to the five percent rate offered under the CPP. To encourage repayment while recognizing the unique circumstances facing CDFIs, the dividend rate increases to nine percent after eight years, compared to after five years under the CPP. CDFIs that participated in the CPP and were in good standing were allowed to exchange their CPP securities for securities under the more favorable terms of this program.

Capital Assistance Program (CAP) and the Supervisory Capital Assessment Program (SCAP)

In 2009, Treasury worked with federal banking regulators to develop a comprehensive "stress test" known as the Supervisory Capital Assessment Program (SCAP). The purpose of the SCAP was to determine the health of the nation's 19 largest bank holding companies with unprecedented transparency and help restore confidence in the banking system. In conjunction with the SCAP, Treasury announced that it would provide capital under TARP through the Capital Assistance Program (CAP) to those institutions that needed additional capital but were unable to raise it through private sources. The CAP closed on November 9, 2009, without making any investments.

For additional information on the bank support programs please visit the OFS website at:

http://www.treasury.gov/initiatives/financial-stability/TARP-Programs/bank-investment-programs/Pages/default.aspx

Credit Market Programs (PPIP, TALF, SBA 7(a))

As the financial crisis reached its peak, banks were not making new loans to businesses, or even to one another. As a result, many businesses could not get loans for new investments, municipalities and state governments could not issue bonds at reasonable rates, and families could not get credit. The securitization markets—which provide financing for credit cards, student loans, auto loans, and other consumer loans as well as small business loans—had basically stopped functioning. OFS launched three programs in 2009 to help unfreeze these markets and bring down the cost of borrowing for families and businesses: the Public-Private Investment Program (PPIP), the Term Asset-Backed Securities Loan Facility (TALF), and the SBA 7(a) Securities Purchase Program. Although the specific goals and implementation methods of each program differed, the overall goal of these three programs was the same—to restart the flow of credit to meet the critical needs of small businesses and consumers.

Public-Private Investment Program

On March 23, 2009, OFS launched the Legacy Securities Public-Private Investment Program (PPIP) to help restart the market for non-agency residential mortgage-backed securities (RMBS) and commercial mortgage-backed securities (CMBS), thereby allowing banks and other financial institutions to re-deploy capital and extend new credit to households and businesses.

The purpose of PPIP was to draw new private capital into the market for legacy RMBS and CMBS by providing financing on attractive terms as well as a matching equity investment from OFS. Using up to $22.1 billion of TARP funds alongside equity capital raised from private investors, PPIP was designed to generate significant purchasing power and demand for troubled RMBS and CMBS. This in turn would help to increase the amount of credit available to consumers and small businesses.

Term Asset-Backed Securities Loan Facility

The Term Asset-Backed Securities Loan Facility (TALF) is a joint OFS-Federal Reserve program that was designed to restart the asset-backed securities (ABS) and commercial mortgage-backed securities (CMBS) markets that had ground to a virtual standstill during the early months of the financial crisis.

Under the TALF, the Federal Reserve Bank of New York (FRBNY) provided non-recourse funding to any qualified borrower that owned eligible collateral. On fixed days each month, borrowers were allowed to request three-year, or in certain cases, five-year TALF loans. If the borrower did not repay the loan, the FRBNY would enforce its rights to the collateral and sell it to TALF, LLC-a special purpose vehicle (SPV) established specifically to purchase and manage these assets. OFS initially committed $20.0 billion in subordinated loans to the SPV but did not directly lend to TALF borrowers.

Small Business Administration 7(a) Securities Purchase Program

OFS launched the Small Business Administration (SBA) 7(a) Securities Purchase Program to help facilitate the recovery of the secondary market for small business loans, and thus help free up credit for small businesses. Under this program, OFS purchased securities comprised of the guaranteed portion of SBA 7(a) loans, which finance a wide range of small business needs, including working capital, machinery, equipment, furniture, and fixtures. OFS invested approximately $367 million in 31 SBA 7(a) securities between March and September 2010. These securities were comprised of 1,001 loans from 17 different industries, including retail, food services, manufacturing, scientific and technical services, healthcare, and educational services. Through its purchases, OFS injected liquidity into this market to help restart the flow of credit, enabling pool assemblers to purchase additional small business loans from loan originators.

For additional information on the credit market programs, please visit the OFS website at: http://www.treasury.gov/initiatives/financial-stability/TARP-Programs/credit-market-programs/Pages/default.aspx

Automotive Industry Financing Program (AIFP)

The Automotive Industry Financing Program (AIFP) was launched in December 2008 to help prevent the disorderly liquidations of General Motors (GM) and Chrysler, and thus significant disruption of the U.S. auto industry. The potential for such a disruption at that time posed a significant risk to financial market stability and threatened the overall economy. It could have also had disastrous consequences for other auto manufacturers and the many suppliers and other businesses that depended on the automotive industry. This could have led to a loss of as many as one million American jobs. Recognizing that both GM and Chrysler were on the verge of collapse, OFS extended loans to both companies and their financing entities.

In 2009, OFS agreed to provide additional funds conditioned on each company and its stakeholders participating in a fundamental restructuring. Sacrifices were made by unions, dealers, creditors and other stakeholders, and the restructurings were achieved through bankruptcy court proceedings in record time. In total OFS disbursed $79.7 billion in loans and equity investments to GM, Chrysler, and General Motors Acceptance Corporation (now known as Ally Financial). As a result, General Motors Company (New GM), Chrysler Group LLC (New Chrysler), and Ally are more competitive and viable companies, supporting American jobs and the economy. Operating results have improved, the industry added jobs, and TARP investments are being repaid.

For additional information on the AIFP, please visit the OFS website at: http://www.treasury.gov/initiatives/financial-stability/TARP-Programs/automotive-programs/Pages/default.aspx

American International Group, Inc. (AIG) Investment Program

On September 15, 2008, Lehman Brothers filed for bankruptcy. This triggered the start of a run on money market funds generally. The day after that, AIG – one of the largest and most complex financial firms in the world – was on the verge of failure. Confidence was already fragile in the financial system as a whole and firms were trying to shore up their balance sheets by selling risky assets, reducing exposure to other financial institutions, and hoarding cash. At the time, AIG was one of the most complex financial firms in the world providing credit for other financial products. When the financial crisis hit, AIG had hundreds of billions of dollars in commitments without the capital and liquid assets to back them up. Millions of people depended on AIG for their life savings and it had a huge presence in many critical financial markets, including municipal bonds. Therefore, with AIG facing potentially fatal liquidity problems and with the crisis threatening to intensify and spread more broadly throughout the economy, OFS and the Federal Reserve provided assistance to AIG. This assistance was provided because the consequences of a company of AIG's size and scope failing at that time, in those circumstances, would have had far-reaching and catastrophic effects for the economy and for American families and businesses.

During this time, the Federal Reserve and OFS took a series of steps to prevent AIG's disorderly failure and mitigate the systemic risks. The initial assistance to AIG was provided by the FRBNY before the passage of EESA and the creation of TARP. After EESA became law, OFS and the FRBNY continued to work together to address the challenges posed by AIG. In 2008 and 2009, OFS funds were used to provide further support to AIG. In fiscal year 2011, OFS, the FRBNY, the trustees of the AIG Credit Facility Trust (the Trust)[1] and AIG completed a restructuring of the assistance provided by OFS

---

[1] The independent trust established to manage the Department of the Treasury's beneficial interest in Series C preferred AIG shares.

and the FRBNY. A series of integrated transactions and corporate actions were executed to accelerate the repayment of U.S. taxpayer funds and to promote AIG's transition from a majority government owned and supported entity to a financially sound and independent entity. Following the restructuring, OFS's total investment in AIG was $67.8 billion.

For additional information on the AIG Investment Program, please visit the Office of Financial Stability website at: http://www.treasury.gov/initiatives/financial-stability/TARP-Programs/aig/Pages/default.aspx

Housing Programs

OFS established several housing programs under TARP to address the historic housing crisis and help struggling homeowners avoid foreclosure wherever possible. These programs have helped homeowners avoid foreclosure and introduced important new reforms for the mortgage servicing industry to help make mortgage modifications become more sustainable and affordable.

Making Home Affordable (MHA)

In early 2009, OFS launched the Making Home Affordable® Program (MHA) to help struggling homeowners avoid foreclosure and stabilize the housing market. MHA is only one part of the Administration's broader efforts to strengthen the housing market. Since its inception, MHA has helped homeowners avoid foreclosure by providing a variety of solutions to modify or refinance their mortgages, get temporary forbearance if they are unemployed, or transition out of homeownership through a short sale or a deed-in-lieu of foreclosure. OFS has committed $29.9 billion under the MHA program.

MHA is aimed at helping homeowners who are experiencing financial hardships to remain in their homes until their financial position improves or they relocate to a more sustainable living situation. In most cases, this means making their monthly mortgage payments more affordable and sustaining those new mortgage terms over time so homeowners can avoid the pain and substantial cost of foreclosure. At the same time, MHA protects the interests of taxpayers by disbursing funds only when transactions are completed and only as long as those contracts remain in place. Therefore, funds will be disbursed over many years.

The cornerstone of MHA is the Home Affordable Modification Program (HAMP), which provides eligible homeowners the opportunity to reduce their monthly mortgage payments to more affordable levels. OFS also introduced additional programs under MHA to help homeowners who are unemployed, "underwater" on their loan (those who owe more on their home than it is currently worth), or are struggling with a second lien. It also includes options for homeowners who would like to transition to a more affordable living situation through a short sale or deed-in-lieu of foreclosure. In early 2012, the Administration announced important enhancements to MHA that expanded the pool of eligible borrowers. Extending the reach of HAMP will assist a broader pool of struggling homeowners, offer support for tenants at risk of displacement due to foreclosure, and provide more robust relief to those who participate. On May 30, 2013, the Administration extended the application deadline for MHA programs to December 31, 2015. Extending the program for two years will benefit many additional families while maintaining clear standards and accountability for the mortgage industry. Taken together, these enhancements will help the housing market recover faster from an unprecedented crisis.

In addition to HAMP, MHA includes several additional programs to help homeowners refinance or address specific types of mortgages, in conjunction with the Federal Housing Administration (FHA), the United States

Department of Agriculture (USDA), and the Department of Veterans Affairs (VA).

Housing Finance Agency (HFA) Innovation Fund for the Hardest Hit Housing Markets (Hardest Hit Fund)

The Administration established the Hardest Hit Fund in February 2010 to provide targeted aid to homeowners in states hit hardest by the economic and housing market downturn. As part of the Administration's overall strategy for restoring stability to housing markets, the Hardest Hit Fund provides funding for state Housing Finance Agencies (HFAs) to develop locally-tailored foreclosure prevention solutions in areas that have been hardest hit by home price declines and high unemployment. From its initial announcement, this program evolved from a $1.5 billion initiative focused on HFAs in the five states with the steepest home price declines and the vast majority of underwater homeowners to a broader-based $7.6 billion initiative encompassing 18 states and the District of Columbia (DC).

Hardest Hit Fund programs vary state to state, but may include such programs as mortgage payment assistance for unemployed or underemployed homeowners, principal reduction to help homeowners get into more affordable mortgages, funding to eliminate homeowners' second lien loans, funding for blight elimination activities, and help for homeowners who are transitioning out of their homes and into more affordable living situations.

For additional information on the housing programs, please visit the OFS website at: http://www.treasury.gov/initiatives/financial-stability/TARP-Programs/housing/Pages/default.aspx

OFS Operational Goals

OFS's Operational Goals were developed by management to achieve our strategic goal to ensure the overall stability and liquidity of the financial system, prevent avoidable foreclosures, and preserve homeownership. The following discussion of OFS operational goals focuses largely on the significant events that occurred during fiscal years 2013 and 2012. A more comprehensive discussion of each program, including its development and prior years' performance, can be found in the TARP Four Year Retrospective which is available at: http://www.treasury.gov/initiatives/financial-stability/reports/Pages/default.aspx

Operational Goal One: Complete the Wind-down of the Investment Programs

Banking Support Programs

OFS disbursed a total of $245.5 billion under the various TARP bank programs. As of September 30, 2013, OFS has collected more than $273.4 billion through repayments, dividends, interest, warrant sales, and other income, representing $27.9 billion in excess of disbursements. No more taxpayer money is being invested in banks under TARP. The final investment under the CPP – the largest bank program under TARP – was made in December 2009. OFS is focused on recovering TARP funds in a manner that continues to promote the nation's financial stability while maximizing returns on behalf of the taxpayers.

Capital Purchase Program

In fiscal year 2013, OFS made substantial progress winding down the CPP according to the three-pronged exit strategy announced in May 2012 and described in further detail below. From inception of the program through September 30, 2013, OFS has received $197.9

billion in CPP repayments/sales, along with $12.0 billion in dividends and interest, and $14.7 billion of proceeds in excess of cost totaling $224.7 billion. As of September 30, 2013, $3.1 billion in CPP gross investments remained outstanding, including 24 institutions that are in bankruptcy or receivership, representing an aggregate investment of $771 million that is currently not collectible.

Under this program, OFS provided capital to 707 financial institutions in 48 states, Puerto Rico, and DC, including more than 450 small and community banks and 22 CDFIs. The largest investment was $25.0 billion and the smallest was $301,000.

OFS received preferred stock or debt in each bank in which it made an investment, as well as warrants. Under the terms of the CPP, participating financial institutions may repay the funds they received at any time, so long as they have the approval of their regulators. OFS cannot demand repayment of CPP preferred stock, nor is OFS's approval required for financial institutions to repay.

OFS announced a three-pronged exit strategy for the program on May 3, 2012. That strategy includes waiting for those banks that are capable of repaying in the near future to repay at par, selling banking investments to private investors through auctions in cases where the bank is not expected to be able to repay in the near future, and, in a limited number of cases, restructuring investments. Throughout fiscal year 2013, OFS continued to implement that exit strategy by periodically selling preferred stock and subordinated debt in CPP participants through both public and private auctions. OFS held 14 auctions with combined proceeds of $1.5 billion during fiscal year 2013 compared to 6 auctions with $1.3 billion in proceeds in fiscal year 2012. During fiscal year 2013 and 2012,

173 and 96 investments were repaid or sold for a total of $4.8 billion and $8.2 billion, respectively.

Another component of OFS's exit strategy for the CPP is to restructure certain investments in limited cases when the terms result in the best return for taxpayers. This is typically done in connection with a merger or the bank's plan to raise new capital and is generally proposed by the bank. OFS agrees to receive cash (sometimes at a discount to the original par value of the investment) or other securities, which can be more easily sold.

Under the CPP, OFS has also received warrants to purchase common shares or other securities from the banks. OFS has followed a policy of disposing of warrants as soon as practicable if no agreement is reached on a repurchase. As of September 30, 2013, OFS has collected $7.9 billion in net proceeds from the sale of warrants since inception. OFS periodically releases a Warrant Disposition Report that provides detail about its sale of warrants. These reports can be found at:

http://www.treasury.gov/initiatives/financial-stability/reports/Pages/Warrant-Disposition-Reports.aspx

Additional information on the CPP, including details on the programs purpose, overview, and status can be found at the following website:

http://www.treasury.gov/initiatives/financial-stability/TARP-Programs/bank-investment-programs/cap/Pages/default.aspx

Targeted Investment Program

OFS completed the wind-down of the TIP in December 2009 when both BofA and Citigroup repaid their TIP investments in full. This resulted in net proceeds of $4.4 billion in excess of disbursements. OFS received $3.0 billion in total TIP dividends during the life of the program. OFS also received warrants from each institution which provided additional returns on the investments. OFS sold the BofA warrants in

fiscal year 2010 for $1.2 billion and the Citigroup warrant in fiscal year 2011 for $190 million. Additional information on TIP, including details on the programs purpose, overview, and status can be found at the following website:

http://www.treasury.gov/initiatives/financial-stability/TARP-Programs/bank-investment-programs/tip/Pages/default.aspx

Asset Guarantee Program

As of September 30, 2013, OFS has fully wound down the AGP and received more than $4.1 billion in proceeds from the AGP without disbursing any claim payments. Additional information on the AGP, including details on the programs purpose, overview, and status can be found at the following website:

http://www.treasury.gov/initiatives/financial-stability/TARP-Programs/bank-investment-programs/agp/Pages/default.aspx

Community Development Capital Initiative

Unlike the CPP, OFS did not take substantial actions during fiscal year 2013 to wind-down the CDCI because of the unique circumstances facing participating institutions. In particular, many CDCI participants lack the same access to capital markets that CPP institutions have, making it more challenging for them to repay their investments.

OFS completed funding through this program in September 2010 with a total investment amount of $570 million for 84 institutions. Of this amount, $363 million (nearly $356 million from principal and nearly $8 million from warrants) represented exchanges by 28 CPP institutions converting into the CDCI. During fiscal years 2013 and 2012, OFS collected a total of $97 million and $14 million, respectively, in repayments, dividends and interest from institutions in the CDCI program. As of September 30, 2013, $475 million in CDCI investments remained outstanding.

OFS will continue to closely monitor the performance of the CDCI and make decisions regarding the program's wind-down at a later date. Additional information on CDCI, including details on the program's purpose, overview, and status can be found at the following website:

http://www.treasury.gov/initiatives/financial-stability/TARP-Programs/bank-investment-programs/cdci/Pages/default.aspx

Credit Market Programs

OFS has now substantially completed the wind-down of all three credit market programs that were launched under TARP. A total of $19.1 billion was disbursed through these programs and a total of $23.5 billion has been collected through September 30, 2013.

Public Private Investment Program

During fiscal year 2013, OFS completed the wind-down of the PPIP. During fiscal year 2013 and 2012, 6 and 2 PPIFs wound down, repaying $5.7 billion and $5.6 billion in debt and $4.1 billion and $1.7 billion in equity capital invested by OFS, respectively. In addition, during fiscal years 2013 and 2012, OFS received $271 million and $1.4 billion in interest and investment income and $1.2 billion and $223 million in net proceeds in excess of costs, respectively from these PPIFs. The final outstanding equity repayment was made in June 2013. As of September 30, 2013, no debt or equity investments are outstanding.

The latest PPIP Quarterly Report includes a summary of PPIP capital activity, portfolio holdings and current pricing, and program and fund performance through September 30, 2013. OFS has published 16 quarterly reports on PPIP to date and expects to provide additional information as the program completes its wind-down. These reports can be found at the following website:

http://www.treasury.gov/initiatives/financial-stability/reports/Pages/Public-Private-Investment-Program-Quarterly-Report.aspx

Term Asset-Backed Securities Loan Facility

OFS originally committed to provide credit protection of up to $20.0 billion in the form of a subordinated loan commitment to TALF, LLC to support up to $200.0 billion of lending by the FRBNY. OFS's commitment was later reduced to $4.3 billion in July 2010 after the program closed to new lending. In June 2012, the Federal Reserve Board and OFS agreed that it was appropriate to further reduce the credit protection OFS provides the TALF, LLC to $1.4 billion from $4.3 billion as the underlying TALF loan portfolio decreased through scheduled and voluntary payments. During 2013 this amount was further reduced to $100 million – the initial loan amount disbursed to fund the TALF, LLC.

During fiscal year 2013, OFS's original disbursed investment through the program was fully repaid with interest. As of September 30, 2013, the balance of outstanding TALF loans provided by FRBNY had declined to $101 million from $1.5 billion on September 30, 2012, due to scheduled and voluntary prepayments by borrowers. All loans that have not been repaid-in-full are current in their payments of principal and interest and are fully collateralized by the residual balance held by the TALF, LLC. As of September 30, 2013, accumulated income earned from investments in TALF, LLC totaled $583 million, all of which occurred during fiscal year 2013.

Additional information on TALF, including details on the programs purpose, overview, and status can be found at the following website:

http://www.treasury.gov/initiatives/financial-stability/TARP-Programs/credit-market-programs/talf/Pages/default.aspx

Small Business Administration 7(a) Securities Purchase Program

During fiscal year 2012, OFS completed the fifth and final disposition of securities within the SBA 7(a) Securities Purchase Program, marking the successful wind-down of the program. OFS collected a total of $376 million through the program. This includes $334 million in sales, $29 million in principal payments, and $13 million in interest payments over the life of the program. These cash collections exceeded OFS's original investment amount by $9 million, excluding purchased accrued interest.

Additional information on SBA 7(a), including details on the program's purpose, overview, and status can be found at the following website:

http://www.treasury.gov/initiatives/financial-stability/TARP-Programs/credit-market-programs/sba7a/Pages/default.aspx

Automotive Industry Financing Program

OFS made substantial progress in the wind-down of the AIFP during fiscal year 2013. In total, OFS disbursed $79.7 billion in loans and equity investments to the auto industry through the AIFP. As of September 30, 2013, OFS has collected $53.3 billion through sales, repayments, dividends and interest under this program.

In December 2012, OFS announced its intent to fully exit its investment in GM within the next 12-15 months. Concurrently with that announcement, GM purchased 200 million shares of GM common stock from OFS, for proceeds of $5.5 billion. In early 2013, OFS commenced the disposition of its remaining 300 million common shares of GM common stock through a series of pre-arranged written trading plans. In June 2013, OFS sold an additional 30 million shares of GM common stock in an underwritten sale in connection with the inclusion of GM common stock in the S&P 500 index for proceeds of $1.0 billion. The total amount collected for fiscal year 2013 was $12.0 billion. As of September 30, 2013, 101 million common shares remained outstanding valued at $3.6 billion. OFS expects to complete the disposition of all remaining shares by the end of 2013.

OFS invested $16.3 billion in Ally Financial (Ally) under TARP. As of September 30, 2013, OFS's outstanding investment in Ally stood at $13.7 billion. Ally made substantial progress in completing the two strategic initiatives OFS previously said were critical to maximize recovery of the investment – the Chapter 11 proceeding of Ally's mortgage subsidiary, Residential Capital LLC ("ResCap"), to address Ally's legacy mortgage liabilities and the sale of its international auto finance operations. During fiscal 2013, Ally, ResCap, and ResCap's major creditors agreed on terms for a plan of reorganization and the settlement of certain claims against Ally. The bankruptcy court has approved this agreement and is expected to rule on the plan of reorganization in early fiscal year 2014. Ally also sold or entered into agreements to sell all of its international auto finance operations for a total of $9.2 billion.

On August 19, 2013, Ally entered into private placement agreements with investors of Ally common stock for an aggregate price of $1.0 billion (later increased to $1.3 billion in November 2013). Concurrently, Ally also entered into agreements with OFS to repurchase all of the outstanding MCP stock and terminate the MCP's Share Adjustment Right (SAR), which provided OFS with the right to receive additional common stock of Ally under certain circumstances if certain events occurred prior to December 30, 2016. Ally repurchased all of its MCP stock from OFS for $5.2 billion in November 2013. In addition, OFS received an additional $725 million for the elimination of the SAR. OFS is actively seeking to wind-down the remaining investment in Ally, which represents approximately 63 percent of Ally's common stock after Ally's private placement completed in November 2013.

Additional information on the AIFP, including details on the programs purpose, overview, and status can be found at the following website:

http://www.treasury.gov/initiatives/financial-stability/TARP-Programs/automotive-programs/Pages/default.aspx

American International Group (AIG) Investment Program

In fiscal year 2013, OFS exited all remaining holdings in AIG. During the financial crisis, the OFS's and the FRBNY's peak support for AIG totaled $182.3 billion. That included $69.8 billion that OFS committed and $112.5 billion committed by the FRBNY, including $22.1 billion of these commitments which were later cancelled. As a result of the combined efforts of AIG, OFS, and the Federal Reserve, $22.7 billion in excess of the total of funds disbursed has been recovered through sales and other income.

In fiscal year 2011, Treasury, including OFS, the FRBNY, the trustees of the AIG Facility Trust (Trust)[2] and AIG completed a restructuring of government investments in AIG. As part of the restructuring, Treasury received 1.7 billion AIG shares (1.1 billion TARP shares and 563 million additional Treasury shares from the trust established by the FRBNY for the benefit of Treasury). Since the restructuring, OFS managed both the TARP and additional Treasury shares and sold them on a pro-rata basis.

During fiscal year 2012, AIG completed the repayment of OFS's preferred interests in the AIG SPVs for proceeds of $9.6 billion. In addition, OFS conducted four offerings that sold a total of 1.2 billion shares of AIG common stock (including 806 million TARP shares) at prices that ranged from $29.00 per share to $32.50 per share. Total proceeds from these sales amounted to $38.2 billion, consisting of $25.2 billion in proceeds to OFS and additional proceeds to the Treasury for the additional Treasury shares of $13.0 billion. The proceeds to OFS from such common stock sales were $9.9 billion less than cost.

During fiscal year 2013, OFS sold its and Treasury's remaining 234 million shares of AIG common stock in two underwritten public offerings for aggregate proceeds of approximately $7.6 billion. The proceeds from these sales consisted of $5.0 billion to OFS and additional proceeds to the Treasury for additional Treasury shares of $2.6 billion. On March 1, 2013, AIG repurchased warrants issued to OFS in 2008 and 2009 for approximately $25 million. OFS disbursed a total of $67.8 billion to AIG, and following this sale, OFS's cumulative net proceeds from repayments, sales, dividends, interest, and other income related to AIG assets totaled $55.3 billion, and OFS has no residual interest in AIG.

OFS sold all the TARP and additional Treasury shares at an average price of $31.18 per share. Because the additional Treasury shares came from the trust, the additional Treasury shares were provided to Treasury at no cost and are not included in the OFS financial statements. The TARP shares had a cost basis of $43.53 per share. However, the figure of $28.73 per share was often referred to as Treasury's "break-even" price for AIG common stock sales in order for Treasury to recover the TARP AIG investment because that number averages the cost over the TARP shares and the additional Treasury shares. Thus, the average price realized was in excess of that break-even price. While TARP recovered less than its total investment, this was offset by the proceeds from the additional Treasury shares of AIG, resulting in overall proceeds exceeding disbursements for Treasury.

---

[2] The independent trust established to manage the Treasury's beneficial interest in preferred AIG shares from the FRBNY.

Operational Goal Two: Continue Helping Families in Need to Avoid Foreclosure

Making Home Affordable (MHA)

Consistent with OFS's goal of continuing to help struggling homeowners find solutions to avoid foreclosure wherever possible, OFS is continuing to implement the MHA program and to reach as many homeowners as possible. As of September 30, 2013, 91 non-GSE servicers are participating in MHA. As of September 30, 2013, OFS has commitments to fund up to $29.9 billion in MHA payments and has disbursed $6.5 billion since inception.

OFS publishes quarterly assessments of servicer performance containing data on compliance with program guidelines as well as program results metrics. OFS believes that these assessments have set the standard for transparency about mortgage servicer efforts to assist homeowners and encourage servicers to improve processes and performance for foreclosure prevention activities.

MHA performance highlights for fiscal year 2013 can be found at:
http://www.treasury.gov/initiatives/financial-stability/reports/Pages/Making-Home Affordable-Program-Performance-Report.aspx.

Additional information on MHA, including details on the programs purpose, overview, and status can be found at the following website:

http://www.treasury.gov/initiatives/financial-stability/TARP-Programs/housing/mha/Pages/default.aspx

Home Affordable Modification Program (HAMP)

The largest program within MHA is the Home Affordable Modification Program (HAMP). HAMP offers responsible homeowners who are at risk of foreclosure the opportunity to obtain reduced monthly mortgage payments that are affordable and sustainable over the long-term.

As of September 30, 2013, approximately 1.3 million homeowners have received permanent modifications through HAMP.[3] This includes modifications on both non-GSE loans (for which the cost is paid by TARP) and GSE loans (for which the cost is paid by the GSEs). Homeowners participating in HAMP have collectively experienced nearly a 40 percent median reduction in their mortgage payments—representing more than $546 per month. MHA has also encouraged the mortgage industry to adopt similar programs that have helped millions more at no cost to taxpayers by establishing standards and best practices for loss mitigation evaluations. As of September 30, 2013, homeowners in HAMP have had their principal reduced by an estimated $22.3 billion.

On May 30, 2013, the Administration extended the application deadline for MHA programs through December 2015 to provide struggling homeowners additional time to access sustainable mortgage relief, and to align the end dates for key assistance programs. OFS and the U.S. Department of Housing and Urban Development (HUD) announced that the new deadline was determined in coordination with the Federal Housing Finance Agency (FHFA) to align with extended deadlines for the Home Affordable Refinance Program (HARP) and the Streamlined Modification Initiative for homeowners with loans owned or guaranteed by Fannie Mae and Freddie Mac.

Housing Finance Agency Innovation Fund for the Hardest Hit Housing Markets (Hardest Hit Fund)

In addition to MHA, OFS also operates the Hardest Hit Fund, which allows participating HFAs in the nation's hardest hit housing and unemployment markets to design innovative,

---

[3] 667,093 of these modifications were OFS funded.

locally-targeted foreclosure prevention programs. As of September 30, 2013, all 19 HFAs are fully operational and have created extensive infrastructures to operate these programs, including selecting and training networks of housing counselors to assist with applications, creating homeowner portals to aid homeowners in applying for assistance, and hiring underwriters and other staff to review and approve applications. The five largest servicers (Bank of America, JPMorgan Chase, Wells Fargo, Citibank, and GMAC) are currently participating in programs in all 19 jurisdictions, primarily through mortgage payment assistance and mortgage loan reinstatement assistance.

As of September 30, 2013, the 19 HFAs have collectively drawn approximately $2.9 billion (38.3 percent) of the $7.6 billion allocated under the program. For fiscal years 2013 and 2012, this program has disbursed $1.4 billion and $861 million, respectively. Each state draws down funds as they are needed, but must have no more than five percent of their allocation on hand before they can draw down additional funds. States have until December 31, 2017, to have entered into agreements with borrowers.

Each HFA submits a quarterly report on the progress of its program. These reports include the states' performance on metrics set by OFS on various aspects of their programs. Direct links to each state's most recent performance report can be found at:

http://www.treasury.gov/initiatives/financial-stability/TARP-Programs/housing/Pages/Program-Documents.aspx.

Additional information on the Hardest Hit Fund, including details on the program's purpose, overview, and status can be found at the following website:

http://www.treasury.gov/initiatives/financial-stability/TARP-Programs/housing/hhf/Pages/default.aspx

FHA Refinance Program

On March 26, 2010, the Department of Housing and Urban Development (HUD) and Department of the Treasury announced enhancements to the Federal Housing Administration Refinance Program (FHA Refinance), designed to make homeownership more affordable for borrowers whose homes are worth less than the remaining amounts on their mortgage loans (negative equity). TARP funds were made available by OFS through an $8.0 billion letter of credit facility, in order to fund a share of the losses experienced by FHA associated with this program (subsequently reduced to $1.0 billion in fiscal year 2013 due to low utilization). As of September 30, 2013, FHA guaranteed 3,015 Refinance loans with a total face value of almost $489 million covered under OFS's letter of credit facility. One default has been realized resulting in $47,840 in claim payments by OFS.

Operational Goal Three: Minimize Cost to Taxpayer

OFS manages TARP investments to minimize costs to taxpayers by managing the timely exit of these investments to reduce taxpayers' exposure, return TARP funds to reduce the federal debt, and continue to replace government assistance with private capital in the financial system. OFS has taken a number of steps during fiscal years 2013 and 2012 to dispose of OFS's outstanding investments in a manner that balances the need to exit these investments as quickly as practicable with maximizing returns for taxpayers. OFS also takes steps to ensure that TARP recipients comply with any TARP-related statutory or contractual obligations such as executive compensation requirements and restrictions on dividend payments.

OFS's exit strategies for TARP investment programs depend on each investment and are subject to market conditions. In disposing of TARP investments, OFS takes a disciplined portfolio approach – reviewing each investment and closely monitoring risk and performance. In addition to repayments by participants, OFS has disposed of investments to third parties through public and private offerings and auctions. Utilizing auctions promotes competition and produces prices that are market-driven.

Risk Assessment

OFS has developed procedures to identify and mitigate investment risk. These procedures are designed to identify TARP recipients that face a heightened financial risk and determine appropriate responses to preserve OFS's investment on behalf of taxpayers, while maintaining financial stability. Specifically, OFS's external asset managers review publicly available information to identify recipients for which pre-tax, pre-provision earnings and capital may be insufficient to offset future losses and maintain required capital. For certain institutions, OFS and its external asset managers engage in heightened monitoring and due diligence that reflects the severity and timing of the challenges.

Compliance

OFS also takes steps to ensure that TARP recipients comply with their TARP-related statutory and contractual obligations. Statutory obligations include executive compensation restrictions. Contractual obligations vary by investment type. For most of OFS's preferred stock investments, TARP recipients must comply with restrictions on payment of dividends and on repurchases of junior securities. Recipients of exceptional assistance (currently GM and Ally) must comply with additional restrictions on executive compensation, lobbying, corporate expenses and internal controls and must provide quarterly compliance reports.

In addition, all mortgage servicers participating in MHA are subject to program guidelines, which require the servicer to offer MHA assistance to all eligible borrowers and to have systems that can process all MHA-eligible loans. Servicers are subject to periodic, on-site

compliance reviews performed by OFS's compliance agent, Making Home Affordable-Compliance (MHA-C), a separate, independent division of Freddie Mac, to ensure that servicers' obligations under MHA requirements are being met. In fiscal year 2011, OFS began publishing quarterly assessments of the largest servicers comprising approximately 89% of the HAMP mortgage servicing market and continued publishing these quarterly assessments throughout fiscal year 2013. These assessments have helped force the industry to improve its practices.

Operational Goal Four: Continue to Operate with the Highest Standards of Transparency, Accountability, and Integrity

To protect taxpayers and help ensure that every dollar is directed toward promoting financial stability, OFS established comprehensive accountability and transparency measures. OFS is committed to operating its investment and housing programs in full view of the public. This includes providing regular and comprehensive information about how TARP funds are being spent, who has received them and on what terms, and how much has been collected to date.

All of this information, along with numerous reports of different frequencies is posted on the Financial Stability section of the Treasury.gov website, which can be found at:

http://www.treasury.gov/initiatives/financial-stability/reports/Pages/default.aspx

These reports include:

- A Daily TARP Update, which features detailed financial data related to each TARP investment program including the status of disbursements and all collections by category;

- A monthly report to Congress that details how TARP funds have been used, the status of recovery of such funds by program, and information on the estimated cost of TARP;
- A monthly report on dividend and interest payments;
- A monthly report on Making Home Affordable;
- A report of each transaction (such as an investment or repayment) within two business days of each transaction;
- A quarterly report on the Hardest Hit Fund;
- A quarterly report on PPIP that provides detailed information on the funds, their investments, and returns. It is typically released within one month after the end of each quarter; and
- A semi-annual report on warrant dispositions.

In addition, OFS regularly publishes data files related to MHA and transaction reports that show activity related to MHA and HHF. The release of the data file fulfills a requirement within the Dodd-Frank Act to make available loan-level data about the program. OFS updates the file monthly and will expand reporting to include newer initiatives that are part of MHA. Researchers interested in using the MHA Data File can access the file and user guide at:

http://www.treasury.gov/initiatives/financial-stability/reports/Pages/mha_publicfile.aspx.

Audited Financial Statements

OFS prepares separate financial statements for TARP on an annual basis. This is the fifth OFS Agency Financial Report (AFR), and includes the audited financial statements for the fiscal years ended September 30, 2013 and September 30, 2012. Additional reports for prior periods are available at:

http://www.treasury.gov/initiatives/financial-stability/reports/Pages/Annual-Agency-Financial-Reports.aspx

In its five years of operation, TARP's financial statements have received five unmodified audit opinions from its auditor, the GAO. OFS also received a Certificate of Excellence in Accountability Reporting (CEAR) from the Association of Government Accountants for fiscal years 2012, 2011, 2010 and the period ending September 30, 2009.

TARP Retrospective Reports and the TARP Tracker

In March 2013, OFS published the *Troubled Asset Relief Program Four Year Retrospective Report - An Update on The Wind-Down of TARP*. This serves as an update to OFS's TARP Three-Year Anniversary report, which was published in October 2011. In October 2010, OFS published the TARP Two Year Retrospective, which contains a comprehensive history of each TARP program. These reports include information on TARP programs and the effects of TARP and additional emergency measures taken by the federal government to stabilize the financial system following the 2008 crisis.

In addition, during fiscal year 2013, OFS launched an expanded version of its existing TARP Tracker, which is an online, interactive tool that allows users to track the flow of TARP funds in greater detail over the lifetime of each individual TARP investment area. The expanded capability allows users to view each investment area separately to get a clearer sense of what has occurred in a particular program, including a scroll of events, major transactions, and legislative actions that have impacted the program.

Readers are invited to refer to these documents at: http://www.treasury.gov/initiatives/financial-stability/reports/Pages/default.aspx

Oversight by Four Separate Agencies

Congress also established four avenues of oversight for TARP:

- The Financial Stability Oversight Board, established by EESA Section 104;
- Specific responsibilities for the GAO as set out in EESA Section 116;
- The Special Inspector General for TARP, established by EESA Section 121; and
- The Congressional Oversight Panel (COP), established by EESA Section 125. COP concluded its operations in accordance with EESA on April 3, 2011.

OFS has productive working relationships with all of these bodies, and cooperates with each oversight agency's effort to produce periodic audits and reports that focus on the many aspects of TARP. Individually and collectively, the oversight bodies' audits and reports have made and continue to make important contributions to the development, strengthening, and transparency of TARP programs.

Congressional Hearings and Testimony

OFS officials have testified in numerous Congressional hearings since TARP was created. Copies of their written testimony are available at:

http://www.treasury.gov/initiatives/financial-stability/news-room/Pages/default.aspx.

Fiscal Year 2012 and 2013 Financial Summary and Cumulative Net Income

OFS's fiscal year 2013 net income from operations of $7.7 billion includes the reported net income related to loans, equity investments, and other credit programs. For the fiscal year ended September 30, 2013, OFS reported net subsidy income for six programs –CPP, CDCI, TALF, PPIP, AGP, and AIFP. These programs collectively reported net subsidy income of $11.9 billion. Also, for the fiscal year ended September 30, 2013, OFS experienced net subsidy cost for two programs – AIG and FHA Refinance Program totaling $34 million. Fiscal year 2013 expenses for the Treasury housing programs under TARP of $4.0 billion and administrative costs of $248 million bring the total reported fiscal year net income from operations to $7.7 billion. For the fiscal year ended September 30, 2012, the net income from operations was $7.7 billion. These net income amounts reported in the financial statements reflect only transactions through September 30, 2013 and September 30, 2012, respectively, and therefore are different than lifetime cost estimates made for budgetary purposes.

Over time the cost of TARP programs will change. As described later in the OFS audited financial statements, these estimates are based in part on currently projected economic factors. These economic factors will likely change, either increasing or decreasing the lifetime cost of TARP.

TARP Program Summary

Table 1 provides a financial summary for TARP programs since its inception on October 3, 2008, through September 30, 2013. For each program, the table provides utilized TARP authority (which includes purchases made, legal commitments to make future purchases, and offsets for guarantees made), the amount actually disbursed, repayments to OFS from program participants or from sales of the investments, write-offs and losses, net outstanding balance as of September 30, 2013, and cash inflows on the investments in the form of dividends, interest or other fees. As of September 30, 2013, $30 billion of the $456.6 billion in purchase and guarantee authority remained unused.

Table 1: TARP Summary[1]
From TARP Inception through September 30, 2013
(Dollars in billions)

	Purchase Price or Guarantee Amounts	Total $ Disbursed	Investment Sales and Repayments	Write-offs and Losses[3]	Out-standing Balance[4]	Received from Invest-ments
Bank Support Programs						
Capital Purchase Program[5]	$ 204.9	$ 204.9	$ (197.9)[6]	$ (3.9)	$ 3.1	$ 26.8
Targeted Investment Program	40.0	40.0	(40.0)	-	-	4.4
Asset Guarantee Program	5.0	-	-	-	-	4.1
Community Development Capital Initiative	0.6	0.6	(0.1)	-	0.5	-
Credit Market Programs						
Public-Private Investment Program	19.6	18.6	(18.6)	-	-	3.8
Term Asset-Backed Securities Loan Facility	0.1	0.1	(0.1)	-	-	0.6
SBA 7(a) Securities Purchase Program	0.4	0.4	(0.4)	-	-	-
Other Programs						
Automotive Industry Financing Program	79.7	79.7	(47.1)	(12.7)	19.9	6.2
American International Group Investment Program[2]	67.8	67.8	(54.3)	(13.5)	:	1.0
Sub-total for Investment Programs	418.1	412.1	(358.5)	(30.1)	23.5	46.9
Treasury Housing Programs under TARP	38.5[7]	9.5	N/A	N/A	N/A	N/A
Total for TARP Program	$ 456.6	$ 421.6	$ (358.5)	$ (30.1)	$ 23.5	$ 46.9

[1] This table shows TARP activity for the period from inception through September 30, 2013, on a cash basis. Received from investments includes dividends and interest income reported in the Statement of Net Cost, and proceeds from sale and repurchases of assets in excess of costs.

[2] The amounts for AIG reflect only the operations of TARP and do not reflect proceeds received from the sale of shares of AIG common stock held by Treasury outside of TARP (additional Treasury shares). For further details, see the discussion of the American International Group Investment Program, beginning on page 14.

[3] Losses represent proceeds less than cost on sales of assets which are reflected in the financial statements within "net proceeds from sales and repurchases of assets in excess of (less than) cost."

[4] Total disbursements less repayments, write-offs and losses do not equal the total outstanding balance because the disbursements for the Treasury housing programs under TARP generally do not require (and OFS does not expect) repayments.

[5] OFS received $31.9 billion in proceeds from sales of Citigroup common stock, of which $25.0 billion is included at cost in investment sales, and $6.9 billion of net proceeds in excess of cost is included in Received from Investments.

[6] Includes $2.2 billion of SBLF refinancing outside of TARP and CDCI exchanges from CPP of $363 million.

[7] Individual obligation amounts are $29.9 billion for the Making Home Affordable Program, $7.6 billion for the Hardest Hit Fund, and $1.0 billion committed for the FHA Refinance Program.

Most TARP funds were used to make investments in preferred stock or to make loans. OFS has generally received dividends on the preferred stock and interest payments on the loans from the institutions participating in TARP programs. These payments represent additional proceeds received on OFS's TARP investments. From inception through September 30, 2013 OFS received a total of $24.2 billion in dividends and interest.

OFS has conducted several sales of its investments in banking institutions as part of its exit strategy for winding down TARP. OFS plans to continue to sell its investments in banks that are not expected to repay OFS in the foreseeable future. These sales are being conducted over time and in stages and include both common and preferred stock and debentures. During fiscal years 2013 and 2012, OFS sold its investments in 113 and 40 banks for combined proceeds of $1.5 billion and $1.3 billion, respectively, through individual public and private auctions. These auctions resulted in net proceeds less than cost of $455 million and $180 million for those investments, respectively.

OFS also received warrants in connection with most of its investments, which provides an opportunity for OFS on behalf of taxpayers to realize additional proceeds on investments. Since the program's inception, through September 30, 2013, OFS has received $9.5 billion in gross proceeds from the disposition of warrants associated with 204 CPP investments, both TIP investments, AGP, and AIG, consisting of (i) $4.0 billion from issuer repurchases at agreed upon values and (ii) $5.5 billion from auctions. TARP's Warrant Disposition Report is posted on the OFS website at the following link:

http://www.treasury.gov/initiatives/financial-stability/reports/Pages/Warrant-Disposition-Reports.aspx.

Summary of TARP Equity Investments

Table 2 provides information on the estimated values of TARP direct loan and equity investments by program, as of the end of fiscal years 2013 and 2012. OFS housing programs under TARP are excluded from the chart because no repayments are expected. The Outstanding Balance column represents the amounts disbursed by OFS relating to the loans and equity investments that were outstanding as of September 30, 2013 and 2012. The Estimated Value of the Investment column represents the present value of net cash inflows that OFS estimates it will receive from the loans and equity investments. These estimates include market risk assumptions. For equity securities, this amount represents fair value. The total difference of $5.6 billion (2013) and $22.9 billion (2012) between the two columns is considered the "subsidy cost allowance" under the Federal Credit Reform Act methods OFS follows for budget and accounting purposes.

See Note 6 in the financial statements for further discussion.

Table 2: Summary of TARP Direct Loans and Equity Investments (Dollars in billions)				
Program	Outstanding Balance as of September 30, 2013[1]	Estimated Value of Investment as of September 30, 2013	Outstanding Balance as of September 30, 2012[1]	Estimated Value of Investment as of September 30, 2012
Bank Support Programs				
Capital Purchase Program	$ 3.1	$ 1.8	$ 8.7	$ 5.7
Community Development Capital Initiative	0.5	0.4	0.6	0.4
Credit Market Programs				
Public-Private Investment Program	0.0	0.0	9.8	10.8
Term Asset-Backed Securities Loan Facility	0.0	0.1	0.1	0.7
Other Programs				
Automotive Industry Financing Program	19.9	15.6	37.2	17.5
American International Group Investment Program	0.0	0.0	6.7	5.1
Total	$ 23.5	$ 17.9	$ 63.1	$ 40.2

[1] Before subsidy cost allowance.

The ultimate cost of TARP will not be known for some time, but it is not expected to change significantly as only a few investment programs remain open with much of the original disbursed investments repaid. The financial performance of the remaining programs will depend on many factors, such as future economic and financial conditions, and the business prospects of specific institutions. The cost estimates are sensitive to slight changes in model assumptions, such as general economic conditions, specific stock price volatility of the entities in which OFS has an equity interest, estimates of expected defaults, and prepayments. Wherever possible, OFS uses market prices of tradable securities to estimate the fair value of TARP investments. Use of market prices was possible for TARP investments that trade in public markets or are closely related to tradable securities. For those TARP investments that do not have direct analogs in private markets, OFS uses internal market-based models to estimate the market value of these investments. All future cash flows are adjusted for market risk. Further details on asset valuation can be found in Note 6 of the Financial Statements.

Comparison of Estimated Lifetime TARP Costs Over Time

Market conditions and the performance of specific financial institutions are critical determinants of TARP's estimated lifetime cost. The changes in OFS estimates since TARP's inception through September 30, 2013, provide a good illustration of this impact. Table 3 provides information on how OFS's estimated lifetime cost of TARP has changed over time. These costs for the non-housing programs fluctuate in large part due to changes in the market prices of common stock for AIG and GM and the estimated value of the Ally stock. This table assumes that all expected investments and disbursements for Treasury housing programs under TARP are completed, and adhere to general government budgeting guidance. This table will not tie to the financial statements since it includes repayments and disbursements expected to be made in the future. Table 3 is consistent with the estimated TARP lifetime cost disclosures on the OFS web site at:

http://www.treasury.gov/initiatives/financial-stability/Pages/default.aspx.

The cost amounts in Table 3 are based on assumptions regarding future events, which are inherently uncertain.

Table 3: Estimated Lifetime TARP Costs (Income)[1]
(Dollars in billions)

Program	Estimated Lifetime Cost (Income) as of September 30				
	2009[5]	2010	2011	2012	2013
Bank Support Programs					
Capital Purchase Program	$ (14.6)	$ (11.2)	$ (13.0)	$ (14.9)	$ (16.1)
Targeted Investment Program	(1.9)	(3.8)	(4.0)	(4.0)	(4.0)
Asset Guarantee Program[2]	(2.2)	(3.7)	(3.7)	(3.9)	(4.0)
Community Development Capital Initiative	0.4	0.3	0.2	0.2	0.1
Credit Market Programs					
Public-Private Investment Program	1.4	(0.7)	(2.4)	(2.4)	(2.7)
Term Asset-Backed Securities Loan Facility	(0.3)	(0.4)	(0.4)	(0.5)	(0.6)
SBA 7(a) Securities Purchase Program	N/A	---	---	---	---
Other Programs					
Automotive Industry Financing Program	34.5	14.7	23.6	24.3	14.7
American International Group Investment Program[3]	56.8	36.9	24.3	15.3	15.2
Subtotal	74.1	32.1	24.6	14.1	2.6
Treasury Housing Programs under TARP[4]	50.0	45.6	45.6	45.6	37.7
Total	$ 124.1	$ 77.7	$ 70.2	$ 59.7	$ 40.3

[1] Estimated program costs (+) or savings (in parentheses) over the life of the program, including interest on re-estimates and excluding administrative costs.

[2] Prior to the termination of the guarantee agreement, OFS guaranteed up to $5.0 billion of potential losses on a $301.0 billion portfolio of loans.

[3] The amounts for AIG reflect only the operations of TARP and do not reflect proceeds received from the sale of shares of AIG common stock held by Treasury outside of TARP (additional Treasury shares). For further details, see the discussion of the American International Group Investment Program, beginning on page 14.

[4] The estimated lifetime cost for Treasury Housing Programs under TARP represent the total commitment except for the FHA Refinance Program, which is accounted for under credit reform. The estimated lifetime cost of the FHA Refinance Program represents the total estimated subsidy cost associated with total obligated amount.

[5] Estimated lifetime cost for 2009 includes funds for projected disbursements and anticipated obligations.

Key Trends/Factors Affecting TARP Future Activities and Ultimate Cost

This section provides additional TARP analytic information and enhanced sensitivity analysis focusing on the remaining TARP dollars/continued taxpayer exposure and what is likely to affect the expected future return. As of September 30, 2013, one TARP program – the AIFP – has more than $5.0 billion still outstanding and remains at the most risk of additional taxpayer loss. Going forward, the collections or costs from the AIFP and the expenditures for Treasury housing programs under TARP are expected to most significantly affect changes to the lifetime cost of TARP.

Automotive Industry Financing Program

As of September 30, 2013, OFS's gross AIFP investments outstanding in GM and Ally Financial totaled $19.9 billion, with an estimated value of $15.6 billion. The future value of OFS's investment in GM will depend on the market price of GM common stock, which is affected by a variety of factors specific to the financial condition and results of operations of GM as well as factors pertaining to the industry and the overall economy, such as the competitiveness of U.S. manufacturers, both domestically and internationally, and macroeconomic conditions (unemployment, Gross Domestic Product growth, etc.) which affect the overall trends in auto sales. The future value of OFS's investment in Ally will depend on industry and macroeconomic factors as well as company-specific factors, including in particular the ability of the company to resolve the bankruptcy of its subsidiary, Residential Capital, LLC (ResCap), in a timely and cost-effective manner, and the proceeds realized from the sale of its international operations.

Treasury Housing Programs Under TARP

OFS committed $38.5 billion to fund Treasury housing programs under TARP. From inception through September 30, 2013, $9.5 billion has been disbursed under these programs, consisting of $6.5 billion for MHA, $2.9 billion for the Hardest Hit Fund, and $0.1 billion for the FHA Refinance Program. If all active modifications made as of September 30, 2013, in association with MHA were to remain current and receive incentives for five years, OFS estimates that $13.3 billion in incentive fees will ultimately be disbursed for MHA alone. The program is continuing to enter into new modifications as the termination date was extended to December 31, 2015. Separately, $7.6 billion has been allocated for the Hardest Hit Fund and $1.0 billion for the FHA Refinance Program.

Sensitivity Analysis

The ultimate value of TARP investments will only be known in time. Realized values will vary from current estimates in part because economic and financial conditions will change. Many TARP investments do not have readily observable values and their values can only be estimated by OFS.

Sensitivity analysis is one way to get some feel for the degree of uncertainty around the OFS estimates. In the analysis reported here, OFS focuses on the AIFP as it is the only remaining program with outstanding investments in excess of $5.0 billion.

AIFP Analysis

The most important inputs to the valuation of OFS's outstanding investments under the AIFP are the market price of New GM common stock and the change in the estimated value of Ally Financial common stock, which is based on the price paid by private investors in November, 2013. Table 4 shows the change in estimated value of OFS outstanding AIFP investments based on a 10 percent increase and 10 percent decrease in the trading price of the New GM common stock and separately a 10 percent increase and 10 percent decrease in the estimated value of the Ally Financial common stock. Figure A shows that the GM securities have recently been trading within the range used in the analysis as well as outside of this range, illustrating the uncertainty around the cost estimates.

Table 4: Impact on AIFP Valuation			
(Dollars in billions)	September 30, 2013 Reported Value for AIFP	Effect of 10% Increase	Effect of 10% Decrease
Impact of GM on AIFP	$15.60	$15.95	$15.25
% change from current	N/A	2.24%	(2.24)%
Impact of Ally (formerly GMAC) on AIFP	$15.60	$16.79	$14.40
% change from current	N/A	7.66%	(7.66)%

Figure A shows the daily closing price of the New GM common stock during fiscal years 2012 and 2013. The closing price for September 30, 2013 was $35.97. The dashed lines represent the high and low price used in the sensitivity analysis.

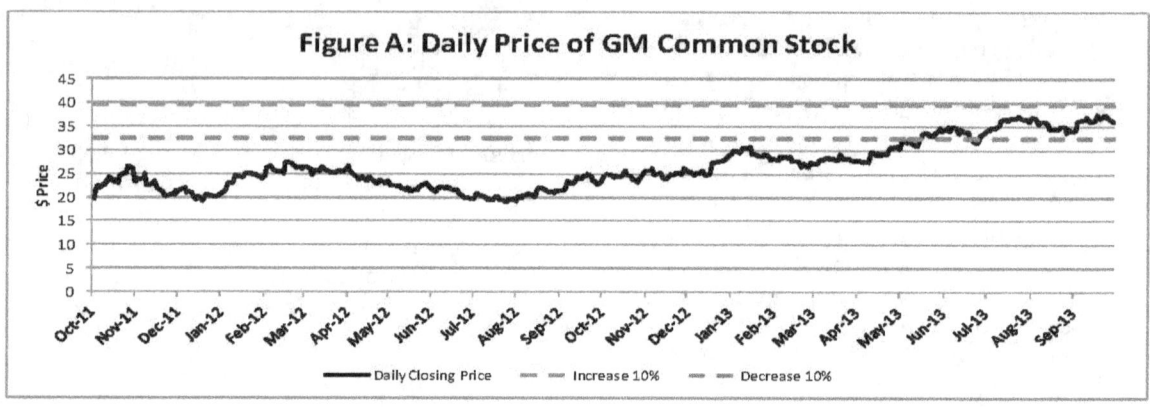

Figure A: Daily Price of GM Common Stock

Systems, Controls, and Legal Compliance

MANAGEMENT ASSURANCE STATEMENT

The Office of Financial Stability's (OFS) management is responsible for establishing and maintaining effective internal control and financial management systems that meet the objectives of the Federal Managers' Financial Integrity Act (FMFIA), 31 U.S.C. 3512(c),(d). OFS has evaluated its management controls, internal controls over financial reporting, and compliance with the federal financial systems standards. As part of the evaluation process, we considered the results of extensive documentation, assessment and testing of controls across OFS, as well as the results of independent audits. We conducted our reviews of internal controls in accordance with FMFIA and Office of Management and Budget (OMB) Circular A-123.

As a result of our reviews, management concludes that the management control objectives described below, taken as a whole, were achieved as of September 30, 2013. Specifically, this assurance is provided relative to Section 2 (internal controls) and 4 (systems controls) of FMFIA. OFS further assures that the financial management systems relied upon by OFS are in substantial compliance with the requirements imposed by the Federal Financial Management Improvement Act (FFMIA).

OFS' internal controls are designed to meet the management objectives established by Treasury and listed below:

(a) Programs achieve their intended results;
(b) Resources are used consistent with overall mission;
(c) Programs and resources are free from waste, fraud, and mismanagement;
(d) Laws and regulations are followed;
(e) Controls are sufficient to minimize any improper or erroneous payments;
(f) Performance information is reliable;
(g) System security is in substantial compliance with all relevant requirements;
(h) Continuity of operations planning in critical areas is sufficient to reduce risk to reasonable levels; and
(i) Financial management systems are in compliance with federal financial systems standards, i.e., FMFIA Section 4 and FFMIA.

In addition, OFS management conducted its assessment of the effectiveness of internal control over financial reporting, which includes safeguarding of assets and compliance with applicable laws and regulations, in accordance with OMB Circular A-123, Management's Responsibility for Internal Control, Appendix A, Internal Control over Financial Reporting. Based on the results of this evaluation, OFS provides unqualified assurance that internal control over financial reporting is appropriately designed and operating effectively as of September 30, 2013, with no related material weaknesses noted.

Sincerely,

Timothy G. Massad
Assistant Secretary for Financial Stability

Internal Control Program

OFS continues to have a high performing internal control program in compliance with the Federal Managers' Financial Integrity Act (FMFIA). FMFIA and OMB Circular A-123, Management's Responsibility for Internal Control, require agencies to evaluate and report on internal controls in place to ensure effectiveness and efficiency of operations, compliance with applicable laws and regulations, and reliability of financial reporting. OFS has completed these rigorous assessments since fiscal year 2009.

OFS has a Senior Assessment Team (SAT) to guide the organization's efforts to meet the statutory and regulatory requirements surrounding a sound system of internal control. OFS's internal control framework is based on the principles of the Committee of Sponsoring Organizations of the Treadway Commission (COSO). The SAT leverages this framework in communicating control objectives across OFS and its third-party service providers. Furthermore, managers throughout OFS are responsible for ensuring that effective internal controls are implemented in their areas of responsibility. Senior management throughout OFS provides assurance statements annually concerning whether there is reasonable assurance that the objectives of internal control are met. Senior management also reports on and takes steps to correct control weaknesses and tracks those weaknesses through resolution.

OFS management believes that maintaining integrity and accountability in all programs and operations is critical to its mission and demonstrates responsible stewardship over assets and resources. It also promotes responsible leadership and maximizes desired program outcomes. OFS has received unmodified opinions from the GAO on its financial statements and internal control over financial reporting since fiscal year 2009, its

first full year of operation. OFS continues to refine its internal controls assessment process to ensure that management can identify risks and deficiencies and make timely corrective actions. The OFS fiscal year 2013 self-assessment of its system of internal controls did not identify any significant deficiencies or material weaknesses.

Information Technology Systems

In fiscal year 2013, OFS continued to utilize and improve the Core Investment Transaction Flow (CITF), TARP's system of record and accounting translation engine. OFS fine-tuned several standardized management reports from CITF to improve their usefulness to management decision-making and added functionality to capture key data elements for use in preparing the financial statements and associated notes.

Other financially relevant systems are supported by financial agents, which provide services to OFS. The financial agency agreements maintained by the Treasury Office of the Fiscal Assistant Secretary in support of OFS require financial agents to design and implement suitably robust security plans and internal control programs, to be reviewed and approved by OFS at least annually.

In addition, OFS utilizes financial systems maintained by Treasury Departmental Offices and various Treasury bureaus. These systems are in compliance with federal financial management systems standards and undergo regular independent audits.

Compliance with the Improper Payments Elimination and Recovery Act (IPERA)

The Improper Payments Elimination and Recovery Act of 2010 (IPERA) requires agencies to review their programs and activities annually to identify those susceptible to significant improper payments. IPERA significantly increases agency payment recapture efforts by requiring reviews of all programs with annual payments of $1 million or more, if cost-effective. IPERA requires agencies to report information on their significant improper payments and recapture audit programs to the President and Congress annually.

The elimination of improper payments is a major focus of OFS senior management. Managers are held accountable for developing and strengthening financial management controls to detect and prevent improper payments, and thereby better safeguard taxpayer dollars. OFS carried out its fiscal year 2013 IPERA review per Treasury-wide guidance and did not assess any programs or activities as susceptible to significant erroneous payments. However, management did identify a number of Making Home Affordable (MHA) investor cost share payments that were erroneously calculated due to data discrepancies between servicer files and the MHA system of record. Data that servicers upload to the MHA system of record is used to calculate these incentive payments. The overall impact of the data errors on incentive payments was immaterial.

In fiscal year 2012 and again in fiscal year 2013, OFS concluded that a payment recapture audit was not cost-effective as all programs were deemed to have a low risk of significant improper payments. For many programs, OFS already has procedures in place to review payments for completeness and accuracy prior to and after disbursement. For the MHA program, nearly 2,000 business rules have been integrated into the MHA system of record to ensure the eligibility, accuracy and appropriateness of incentive payments. Management leverages OFS's extensive internal control testing results or other compliance activities to corroborate risk assessment results, as well as the Bureau of the Fiscal Service's testing results over administrative disbursements.

On April 12, 2012, OMB issued Memorandum M-12-11 "Reducing Improper Payments through the 'Do Not Pay List,'" based on a Directive provided by the President in June 2010. The President directed agencies to "review current pre-payment and pre-award procedures and ensure that a thorough review of available databases with relevant information on eligibility occurs before the release of any Federal funds." In order to achieve this mission, the President directed the creation of a single point of entry through which agencies would access relevant data before determining eligibility for Federal funding commonly referred to as the "Do Not Pay List." Prior to the release of this Directive, OFS already had strong controls in place to help ensure payment eligibility. During fiscal year 2013, OFS implemented the "Do Not Pay List" solution to monitor administrative disbursements and, to date, the "Do Not Pay" Business Center has not identified any potential OFS improper payments. Going forward, OFS will, as appropriate, integrate additional "Do Not Pay List" functionality into its operations.

Areas for Improvement

Over the next year, OFS management will focus on maintaining its internal control environment in several key areas as follows:

- As programs continue to wind-down, OFS will remain vigilant to maintain effective processes and controls. OFS management will take steps to sustain adequate segregation of duties and the right level of institutional knowledge among remaining staff as the size of the organization decreases.

- Third-party service providers will continue to support critical services as programs continue to wind-down. OFS will oversee and monitor closely these third parties to safeguard OFS resources and help ensure the operational efficiency of programs and processes.

- As OFS programs conclude and staff continues to decrease, OFS plans to streamline the number and depth of policies and procedures to make them more efficient and reduce the maintenance burden. OFS will manage this process through the

SAT to ensure that any resulting risk is minimal and controlled.

- OFS has developed information technology capabilities to increase efficiency and automate manual processes. Continuing to leverage existing information technology assets will help reduce risks associated with human error. In fiscal year 2014, OFS will work to right-size the information technology environment to better align with the decreasing level of activity due to the ongoing wind down of OFS programs.

Limitations of the Financial Statements

The principal financial statements have been prepared to report the financial position and results of operations of OFS's TARP programs, consistent with the requirements of 31 U.S.C. 3515(b). While the statements have been prepared from the books and records of OFS and the Department of the Treasury in accordance with section 116 of EESA and Generally Accepted Accounting Principles (GAAP) for Federal entities and the formats prescribed by OMB, the statements are in addition to the financial reports used to monitor and control budgetary resources which are prepared from the same books and records.

The statements should be read with the realization that they are for a component of the U.S. Government, a sovereign entity.

t

MESSAGE FROM THE CHIEF FINANCIAL OFFICER (CFO)

The Office of Financial Stability's (OFS) Agency Financial Report for fiscal year 2013 provides readers information on financial results relating to the Troubled Asset Relief Program (TARP) as required by the Emergency Economic Stabilization Act (EESA) of 2008 and other laws. It is a critical part of our efforts to ensure the highest level of transparency and accountability to the American people.

For fiscal year 2013, the Government Accountability Office (GAO) provided OFS unmodified audit opinions on the fair presentation of our financial statements and the effectiveness of our internal control over financial reporting. In addition, the auditors determined that we had no material weaknesses or significant deficiencies relating to internal control over our accounting and financial reporting processes. Since the inception of TARP in 2009, the program has consistently received unmodified audit opinions – a remarkable achievement for a start-up organization with complex programs.

I would like to acknowledge senior management's commitment to good governance as well as the discipline, transparency, and care exhibited by OFS employees in creating and executing our organization's policies and procedures. We were honored to have received the Certificate of Excellence in Accountability Reporting (CEAR) award from the Association of Government Accountants for each of the four periods from inception through the fiscal year 2012.

For fiscal year 2013, net income from operations was $7.7 billion, resulting in a cumulative net cost of operations of $12.6 billion since inception. Cumulative net cost of operations consists of (1) total net subsidy cost of $1.6 billion, and (2) housing costs and administrative costs of $9.7 billion and $1.3 billion, respectively. Total cumulative net subsidy cost consists of net subsidy income from the CPP, TIP, AGP, PPIP, SBA and TALF investments totaling $27.4 billion, offset primarily by net subsidy cost from investments in AIG of $15.2 billion, and automobile company investments of $13.7 billion.

During fiscal year 2013, OFS collected a total of $35.9 billion through repayments, sales, dividends, and other receipts. OFS's gross outstanding loan and equity investment balance as of September 30, 2013 was $23.5 billion, comprising $19.9 billion in AIFP, $3.1 billion in CPP, and the remainder in CDCI and TALF. OFS is committed to exiting investments in a timely manner while maximizing collections on behalf of the taxpayer.

In fiscal year 2013, OFS continued to maintain rigorous internal control processes around transaction processing, disbursements, collections, and financial reporting. OFS further standardized and automated its subsidiary ledger reporting supporting the validation and reconciliation of financial data and continued enhancements to various financial reports. In the upcoming fiscal year, OFS will seek to streamline and simplify internal control processes in order to accommodate the continued wind-down of TARP investment programs.

I feel fortunate to play a role in the continuing tradition of sound fiscal stewardship at OFS. This organization recognizes the importance of a robust control environment and will continue to uphold the highest standards of integrity as we carry out our fiduciary responsibilities to the American people.

Sincerely,

Lorenzo Rasetti

Lorenzo Rasetti
Chief Financial Officer

GOVERNMENT ACCOUNTABILITY OFFICE AUDITOR'S REPORT

U.S. GOVERNMENT ACCOUNTABILITY OFFICE

441 G St. N.W.
Washington, DC
20548

Independent Auditor's Report

To the Assistant Secretary for Financial Stability

In our audits of the fiscal years 2013 and 2012 financial statements of the Troubled Asset Relief Program (TARP), which is implemented by the Office of Financial Stability (OFS),[1] we found

- the OFS financial statements for TARP as of and for the fiscal years ended September 30, 2013, and 2012, are presented fairly, in all material respects, in accordance with U.S. generally accepted accounting principles;
- OFS maintained, in all material respects, effective internal control over financial reporting for TARP as of September 30, 2013; and
- no reportable noncompliance for fiscal year 2013 with provisions of applicable laws, regulations, contracts, and grant agreements we tested.

The following sections discuss in more detail (1) our report on the financial statements and on internal control over financial reporting, which includes two emphasis of matters related to certain factors affecting the valuation of TARP direct loans, equity investments and asset guarantee program and the TARP reporting entity, and required supplementary information (RSI) and other information included with the financial statements; (2) our report on compliance with laws, regulations, contracts, and grant agreements; and (3) agency comments. In addition to our responsibility to audit OFS's annual financial statements for TARP, we also are required under the Emergency Economic Stabilization Act of 2008 (EESA)[2] to report at least every 60 days on the findings resulting from our oversight of the actions taken under TARP.[3] This report responds to both of these requirements. We have issued numerous other reports on TARP in connection with this 60-day reporting responsibility, which can be found on GAO's website at http://www.gao.gov.

---

[1] Section 101 of the Emergency Economic Stabilization Act of 2008, Pub. L. No. 110-343, div. A, 122 Stat 3765, 3767 (Oct. 3, 2008), *classified at* 12 U.S.C. § 5211, established OFS within the Department of the Treasury (Treasury) to implement TARP.

[2] EESA is classified, in part, as amended, as sections 5201 through 5261 of Title 31 of the United States Code. Section 116(b) of EESA, 12 U.S.C. § 5226(b), requires that Treasury annually prepare and submit to Congress and the public audited fiscal year financial statements for TARP that are prepared in accordance with generally accepted accounting principles. Section 116(b) further requires that GAO audit TARP's financial statements annually in accordance with generally accepted auditing standards.

[3] EESA § 116(a)(3), 12 U.S.C. § 5226(a)(3).

Report on the Financial Statements and on Internal Control over Financial Reporting

In accordance with EESA, we have audited the OFS financial statements for TARP. The OFS financial statements for TARP comprise the balance sheets as of September 30, 2013, and 2012; the related statements of net cost of operations, changes in net position, and budgetary resources for the fiscal years then ended; and the related notes to the financial statements. We also have audited OFS's internal control over financial reporting for TARP as of September 30, 2013, based on criteria established under 31 U.S.C. § 3512(c), (d), commonly known as the Federal Managers' Financial Integrity Act (FMFIA).

We conducted our audits in accordance with U.S. generally accepted government auditing standards. We believe that the audit evidence we obtained is sufficient and appropriate to provide a basis for our audit opinions.

Management's Responsibility

OFS management is responsible for (1) the preparation and fair presentation of these financial statements in accordance with U.S. generally accepted accounting principles; (2) preparing, measuring, and presenting the RSI in accordance with U.S. generally accepted accounting principles; (3) preparing and presenting other information included in documents containing the audited financial statements and auditor's report, and ensuring the consistency of that information with the audited financial statements and the RSI; (4) maintaining effective internal control over financial reporting, including the design, implementation, and maintenance of internal control relevant to the preparation and fair presentation of financial statements that are free from material misstatement, whether due to fraud or error; (5) evaluating the effectiveness of internal control over financial reporting based on the criteria established under FMFIA; and (6) providing its assertion about the effectiveness of internal control over financial reporting as of September 30, 2013, based on its evaluation, included in the accompanying Management's Report on Internal Control over Financial Reporting in appendix I.

Auditor's Responsibility

Our responsibility is to express an opinion on these financial statements and an opinion on OFS's internal control over financial reporting for TARP based on our audits. U.S. generally accepted government auditing standards require that we plan and perform the audits to obtain reasonable assurance about whether the financial statements are free from material misstatement, and whether effective internal control over financial reporting was maintained in all material respects. We are also responsible for applying certain limited procedures to the RSI and other information included with the financial statements.

An audit of financial statements involves performing procedures to obtain audit evidence about the amounts and disclosures in the financial statements. The procedures selected depend on the auditor's judgment, including the auditor's assessment of the risks of material misstatement of the financial statements, whether due to fraud or error. In making those risk assessments, the auditor considers internal control relevant to the entity's preparation and fair presentation of the financial statements in order to design audit procedures that are appropriate in the circumstances. An audit of financial statements also involves evaluating the appropriateness of the accounting policies used and the reasonableness of significant accounting estimates made by management, as well as evaluating the overall presentation of the financial statements. An audit of internal control over financial reporting includes obtaining an understanding of internal control over financial reporting, assessing the risk that a material weakness exists, evaluating the design and operating effectiveness of internal control over financial reporting based on the assessed risk, and testing relevant internal control over financial reporting. Our audit of internal control also considered the entity's process for evaluating and reporting on internal control over financial reporting based on criteria established under FMFIA. Our audits also included performing such other procedures as we considered necessary in the circumstances.

We did not evaluate all internal controls relevant to operating objectives as broadly established under FMFIA, such as those controls relevant to preparing performance information and ensuring efficient operations. We limited our internal control testing to testing controls over financial reporting. Our internal control testing was for the purpose of expressing an opinion on whether effective internal control over financial reporting was maintained, in all material respects. Consequently, our audit may not identify all deficiencies in internal control over financial reporting that are less severe than a material weakness.[4]

Definitions and Inherent Limitations of Internal Control over Financial Reporting

An entity's internal control over financial reporting is a process effected by those charged with governance, management, and other personnel, the objectives of which are to provide reasonable assurance that (1) transactions are properly recorded, processed, and summarized to permit the preparation of financial statements in accordance with U.S. generally accepted accounting principles, and assets are safeguarded against loss from unauthorized acquisition, use, or disposition, and (2) transactions are executed in accordance with laws governing the use of budget authority and with other applicable laws, regulations, contracts, and grant agreements that could have a direct and material effect on the financial statements.

Because of its inherent limitations, internal control over financial reporting may not prevent, or detect and correct, misstatements due to fraud or error. We also caution that projecting any evaluation of effectiveness to future periods is subject to the risk that controls may become inadequate because of changes in conditions, or that the degree of compliance with the policies or procedures may deteriorate.

Opinion on Financial Statements

In our opinion, OFS's financial statements for TARP present fairly, in all material respects, TARP's financial position as of September 30, 2013, and 2012, and its net cost of operations, changes in net position, and budgetary resources for the fiscal years then ended in accordance with U.S. generally accepted accounting principles.

Emphasis of Matters

Valuation of TARP's Direct Loans, Equity Investments, and Asset Guarantee Program

As discussed in notes 2 and 6 to OFS's financial statements for TARP, the valuation of TARP's direct loans, equity investments, and asset guarantee program is based on estimates using economic and financial credit subsidy models. The estimates use entity-specific as well as relevant market data as the basis for assumptions about future performance, and incorporate an

---

[4]A material weakness is a deficiency, or combination of deficiencies, in internal control over financial reporting, such that there is a reasonable possibility that a material misstatement of the entity's financial statements will not be prevented, or detected and corrected, on a timely basis. A deficiency in internal control exists when the design or operation of a control does not allow management or employees, in the normal course of performing their assigned functions, to prevent, or detect and correct, misstatements on a timely basis.

adjustment for market risk to reflect the variability around any unexpected losses. In valuing the direct loans, the equity investments, and the asset guarantee program, OFS management considered and selected assumptions and data that it believed provided a reasonable basis for the estimated subsidy allowance and related subsidy cost or income reported in the financial statements.[5] However, there are numerous factors that affect these assumptions and estimates, which are inherently subject to substantial uncertainty arising from the likelihood of future changes in general economic, regulatory, and market conditions. The estimates have an added uncertainty resulting from the unique nature of certain TARP assets. As such, there will be differences between the net estimated values of the direct loans, equity investments, and asset guarantee program as of September 30, 2013, and 2012 (which totaled $17.9 billion and $41.2 billion, respectively) and the amounts that OFS will ultimately realize from these assets, and such differences may be material. These differences will also affect TARP's ultimate cost. Further, TARP's ultimate cost will change as OFS continues to incur costs relating to its Treasury Housing Programs.[6]

TARP Reporting Entity

As discussed in note 1 to the financial statements, while OFS's financial statements for TARP reflect activity of OFS in implementing TARP, including providing resources to various entities to help stabilize the financial markets, the statements do not include the assets, liabilities, or results of operations of these entities in which OFS has a significant equity interest. According to OFS officials, OFS's investments were not made to engage in the business activities of the respective entities, and OFS has determined that none of these entities meet the criteria for a federal entity.

Our opinion on OFS's financial statements for TARP is not modified with respect to these matters.

Opinion on Internal Control over Financial Reporting

In our opinion, OFS maintained, in all material respects, effective internal control over financial reporting for TARP as of September 30, 2013, based on criteria established under FMFIA.

During our fiscal year 2013 audit, we identified deficiencies in OFS's internal control over financial reporting that we do not consider to be material weaknesses or significant deficiencies.[7] Nonetheless, these deficiencies warrant OFS management's attention. We have communicated these matters to OFS management and, where appropriate, will report on them separately.

---

[5]The subsidy cost or income is composed of (1) the change in the subsidy cost allowance, net of write-offs; (2) net intragovernmental interest cost; (3) certain inflows from the direct loans and equity investments (e.g., dividends, interest, net proceeds from sales and repurchases of assets in excess of cost, and other realized fees); and (4) the change in the estimated discounted net cash flows related to other credit programs (asset guarantee program and Federal Housing Administration refinance program).

[6]The Dodd-Frank Wall Street Reform and Consumer Protection Act, Pub. L. No. 111-203, title XIII, § 1302, 124 Stat. 1376, 2133 (July 21, 2010), (1) limited Treasury's authority to purchase or guarantee troubled assets to a maximum of $475 billion; (2) changed this limit to a cap on all purchases and guarantees made without regard to subsequent sale, repayment, or cancellation of assets or guarantees; and (3) prohibited Treasury, under EESA, from incurring any obligations for a program or initiative unless the program or initiative had already been initiated prior to June 25, 2010.

[7]A significant deficiency is a deficiency, or a combination of deficiencies, in internal control that is less severe than a material weakness, yet important enough to merit attention by those charged with governance.

Other Matters

Required Supplementary Information

U.S. generally accepted accounting principles issued by the Federal Accounting Standards Advisory Board (FASAB) require that RSI be presented to supplement the financial statements.[8] Although not a part of the financial statements, FASAB considers this information to be an essential part of financial reporting for placing the financial statements in appropriate operational, economic, or historical context. We have applied certain limited procedures to the RSI in accordance with U.S. generally accepted government auditing standards, which consisted of inquiries of management about the methods of preparing the RSI and comparing the information for consistency with management's responses to the auditor's inquiries, the financial statements, and other knowledge we obtained during the audit of the financial statements, in order to report omissions or material departures from FASAB guidelines, if any, identified by these limited procedures. We did not audit and we do not express an opinion or provide any assurance on the RSI because the limited procedures we applied do not provide sufficient evidence to express an opinion or provide any assurance.

Other Information

OFS's other information contains a wide range of information, some of which is not directly related to the financial statements.[9] This information is presented for purposes of additional analysis and is not a required part of the financial statements or RSI. We read the other information included with the financial statements in order to identify material inconsistencies, if any, with the audited financial statements. Our audit was conducted for the purpose of forming an opinion on OFS's financial statements for TARP. We did not audit and do not express an opinion or provide any assurance on the other information.

Report on Compliance with Laws, Regulations, Contracts, and Grant Agreements

In connection with our audits of OFS's financial statements for TARP, we tested compliance with selected provisions of applicable laws, regulations, contracts, and grant agreements consistent with our auditor's responsibility discussed below. We caution that noncompliance may occur and not be detected by these tests. We performed our tests of compliance in accordance with U.S. generally accepted government auditing standards.

Management's Responsibility

OFS management is responsible for complying with laws, regulations, contracts, and grant agreements applicable to OFS.

---

[8]RSI is comprised of "Management's Discussion and Analysis" and the "Combined Statement of Budgetary Resources" that are included with the financial statements.

[9]Other information is comprised of information included with the financial statements, other than RSI and the auditor's report.

Auditor's Responsibility

Our responsibility is to test compliance with selected provisions of laws, regulations, contracts, and grant agreements applicable to OFS that have a direct effect on the determination of material amounts and disclosures in the TARP financial statements, and perform certain other limited procedures. Accordingly, we did not test compliance with all laws, regulations, contracts, and grant agreements applicable to OFS.

Results of Our Tests for Compliance with Laws, Regulations, Contracts, and Grant Agreements

Our tests for compliance with selected provisions of applicable laws, regulations, contracts, and grant agreements disclosed no instances of noncompliance for fiscal year 2013 that would be reportable under U.S. generally accepted government auditing standards. However, the objective of our tests was not to provide an opinion on compliance with laws, regulations, contracts, and grant agreements applicable to OFS. Accordingly, we do not express such an opinion.

Intended Purpose of Report on Compliance with Laws, Regulations, Contracts, and Grant Agreements

The purpose of this report is solely to describe the scope of our testing of compliance with selected provisions of applicable laws, regulations, contracts, and grant agreements, and the results of that testing, and not to provide an opinion on compliance. This report is an integral part of an audit performed in accordance with U.S. generally accepted government auditing standards in considering compliance. Accordingly, this report on compliance with laws, regulations, contracts, and grant agreements is not suitable for any other purpose.

Agency Comments

In commenting on a draft of this report, the Assistant Secretary for Financial Stability stated that OFS is proud to receive unmodified opinions on its financial statements and its internal control over financial reporting. He also stated that OFS is committed to maintaining the high standards and transparency reflected in these audit results. The complete text of OFS's comments is reprinted in its entirety in appendix II.

Gary T. Engel

Gary T. Engel
Director
Financial Management and Assurance

December 5, 2013

Appendix I: Management's Report on Internal Control Over Financial Reporting

DEPARTMENT OF THE TREASURY
WASHINGTON, D.C. 20220

ASSISTANT SECRETARY

Management's Report on Internal Control Over Financial Reporting

The Office of Financial Stability's (OFS) internal control over financial reporting (for TARP) is a process effected by those charged with governance, management, and other personnel, the objectives of which are to provide reasonable assurance that (1) transactions are properly recorded, processed, and summarized to permit the preparation of financial statements in accordance with U.S. generally accepted accounting principles, and assets are safeguarded against loss from unauthorized acquisition, use, or disposition; and (2) transactions are executed in accordance with laws governing the use of budget authority and with other applicable laws, regulations, contracts, and grant agreements that could have a direct and material effect on the financial statements.

OFS management is responsible for maintaining effective internal control over financial reporting, including the design, implementation, and maintenance of internal control relevant to the preparation and fair presentation of financial statements that are free from material misstatement, whether due to fraud or error. OFS management evaluated the effectiveness of OFS's internal control over financial reporting as of September 30, 2013, based on the criteria established under 31 U.S.C. 3512(c), (d) (commonly known as the Federal Managers' Financial Integrity Act).

Based on that evaluation, we conclude that, as of September 30, 2013, OFS's internal control over financial reporting was effective.

Office of Financial Stability

Timothy G. Massad
Assistant Secretary for Financial Stability

Lorenzo Rasetti
Chief Financial Officer

December 5, 2013

Appendix II: OFS Response to Auditor's Report

DEPARTMENT OF THE TREASURY
WASHINGTON, D.C. 20220

ASSISTANT SECRETARY

December 5, 2013

Mr. Gary T. Engel
Director, Financial Management and Assurance
U.S. Government Accountability Office
441 G Street, N.W.
Washington, DC 20548

Dear Mr. Engel:

We have reviewed the Independent Auditor's Report concerning your audit of the Office of Financial Stability's (OFS) fiscal year 2013 financial statements. OFS is proud to receive unmodified opinions on our financial statements and our internal controls over financial reporting.

We appreciate the professionalism and commitment demonstrated by your staff throughout the audit process. The process was valuable for us and resulted in concrete improvements in our operations and financial management efforts.

OFS is committed to maintaining the high standards and transparency reflected in these audit results as we carry out our responsibilities for managing the Troubled Asset Relief Program.

Sincerely,

Timothy G. Massad
Assistant Secretary for Financial Stability

FINANCIAL STATEMENTS

The Office of Financial Stability (OFS) prepares financial statements for the Troubled Asset Relief Program (TARP) as a critical aspect of ensuring the accountability and stewardship for the public resources entrusted to it and as required by Section 116 of the Emergency Economic Stabilization Act of 2008 (EESA). Preparation of these statements is also an important part of the OFS's financial management goal of providing accurate and reliable information that may be used to assess performance and allocate resources. The OFS management is responsible for the accuracy and propriety of the information contained in the financial statements and the quality of internal controls. The statements are, in addition to other financial reports, used to monitor and control budgetary resources. The OFS prepares these financial statements from its books and records in conformity with the accounting principles generally accepted in the United States for federal entities and the formats prescribed by the Office of Management and Budget (OMB).

While these financial statements reflect activity of the OFS in executing its programs, including providing resources to various entities to help stabilize the financial markets, they do not include, as more fully discussed in Note 1, the assets, liabilities, or results of operations of commercial entities in which the OFS has a significant equity interest.

The Balance Sheet summarizes the OFS assets, liabilities and net position as of September 30, 2013 and 2012. Intragovernmental assets and liabilities resulting from transactions between federal agencies are presented separately from assets and liabilities resulting from transactions with the public.

The Statement of Net Cost presents the net cost of (income from) operations for the years ended September 30, 2013 and 2012.

The Statement of Changes in Net Position presents the change in OFS's net position for two components, Cumulative Results of Operations and Unexpended Appropriations, for the years ended September 30, 2013 and 2012. The ending balances of both components of net position are also reported on the Balance Sheet.

The Statement of Budgetary Resources provides information about funding and availability of budgetary resources and the status of those resources for the years ended September 30, 2013 and 2012.

Office of Financial Stability - Troubled Asset Relief Program
BALANCE SHEET
As of September 30, 2013 and 2012

Dollars in Millions		2013		2012
ASSETS				
Intragovernmental Assets:				
Fund Balance with Treasury (Note 3)	$	53,240	$	75,495
Asset Guarantee Program (Note 6)		-		967
Other		1		1
Total Intragovernmental Assets		53,241		76,463
Cash on Deposit for Housing Program (Note 4)		50		50
Direct Loans and Equity Investments, Net (Note 6)		17,869		40,231
Total Assets	$	71,160	$	116,744
LIABILITIES				
Intragovernmental Liabilities:				
Accounts Payable and Other Liabilities	$	1	$	2
Due to the General Fund (Note 7)		8,139		9,714
Principal Payable to the Bureau of the Fiscal Service (Note 8)		11,949		52,828
Total Intragovernmental Liabilities		20,089		62,544
Accounts Payable and Other Liabilities		87		87
Liabilities for Treasury Housing Programs Under TARP:				
FHA-Refinance Program (Notes 5 and 6)		9		7
Making Home Affordable Program and Hardest Hit Fund (Note 5)		263		241
Total Liabilities	$	20,448	$	62,879
Commitments and Contingencies (Note 9)		-		-
NET POSITION				
Unexpended Appropriations	$	50,663	$	54,572
Cumulative Results of Operations		49		(707)
Total Net Position	$	50,712	$	53,865
Total Liabilities and Net Position	$	71,160	$	116,744

The accompanying notes are an integral part of these financial statements.

Office of Financial Stability - Troubled Asset Relief Program
STATEMENT OF NET COST
For the Years Ended September 30, 2013 and 2012

Dollars in Millions	2013	2012
STRATEGIC GOAL: TO ENSURE THE OVERALL STABILITY AND LIQUIDITY OF THE FINANCIAL SYSTEM, PREVENT AVOIDABLE FORECLOSURES AND PRESERVE HOME OWNERSHIP		
Gross Cost of (Income from) Operations:		
Program Subsidy Cost (Income) (Note 6)		
Direct Loan and Equity Investment Programs	$ (11,794) $	(10,778)
Other Credit Programs	(116)	(201)
Total Program Subsidy Cost (Income)	**(11,910)**	**(10,979)**
Interest Expense on Borrowings from the Bureau of the Fiscal Service (Note 10)	856	2,252
Treasury Housing Programs Under TARP (Note 5)	3,961	2,963
Administrative Cost	248	268
Total Gross Cost of (Income from) Operations	**(6,845)**	**(5,496)**
Earned Revenue:		
Dividend and Interest Income - Programs (Note 6)	(1,292)	(2,733)
Interest Income on Financing Account (Note 10)	(235)	(605)
Subsidy Allowance Amortization (Note 10)	671	1,086
Total Earned Revenue	**(856)**	**(2,252)**
Total Net Cost of (Income from) Operations	**$ (7,701) $**	**(7,748)**

The accompanying notes are an integral part of these financial statements.

Office of Financial Stability - Troubled Asset Relief Program
STATEMENT OF CHANGES IN NET POSITION
For the Years Ended September 30, 2013 and 2012

| | 2013 | | 2012 | |
| | Unexpended Appropriations | Cumulative Results of Operations | Unexpended Appropriations | Cumulative Results of Operations |
Dollars in Millions				
Beginning Balances	$ 54,572	$ (707)	$ 57,544	$ (27,836)
Budgetary Financing Sources				
Appropriations Received	788	-	27,593	-
Appropriations Used	(4,697)	4,697	(30,565)	30,565
Other Financing Sources	-	(11,642)	-	(11,184)
Total Financing Sources	(3,909)	(6,945)	(2,972)	19,381
Net (Cost of) Income from Operations	-	7,701	-	7,748
Net Change	(3,909)	756	(2,972)	27,129
Ending Balances	$ 50,663	$ 49	$ 54,572	$ (707)

The accompanying notes are an integral part of these financial statements.

Office of Financial Stability - Troubled Asset Relief Program

STATEMENT OF BUDGETARY RESOURCES
For the Years Ended September 30, 2013 and 2012

Dollars in Millions	2013 Budgetary Accounts	2013 Nonbudgetary Financing Accounts	2012 Budgetary Accounts	2012 Nonbudgetary Financing Accounts
BUDGETARY RESOURCES				
Unobligated Balance Brought Forward, October 1	$ 14,350	$ 17,631	$ 14,166	$ 21,143
Recoveries of Prior-Year Unpaid Obligations	7,246	4,941	146	6,114
Borrowing Authority Withdrawn	-	(2,611)	-	(5,832)
Actual Repayments of Debt, Prior-Year Balances	-	(17,738)	-	(19,900)
Unobligated Balance from Prior-Year Budget Authority, Net	21,596	2,223	14,312	1,525
Appropriations	788	-	27,593	-
Borrowing Authority	-	208	-	2,659
Spending Authority from Offsetting Collections	1	13,131	-	21,695
TOTAL BUDGETARY RESOURCES (Note 11)	**$ 22,385**	**$ 15,562**	**$ 41,905**	**$ 25,879**
STATUS OF BUDGETARY RESOURCES				
Obligations Incurred	$ 779	$ 14,100	$ 27,555	$ 8,248
Unobligated Balance:				
Apportioned	11	668	41	3,946
Unapportioned	21,595	794	14,309	13,685
Total Unobligated Balance	21,606	1,462	14,350	17,631
TOTAL STATUS OF BUDGETARY RESOURCES	**$ 22,385**	**$ 15,562**	**$ 41,905**	**$ 25,879**
CHANGE IN OBLIGATED BALANCES				
Unpaid Obligations:				
Unpaid Obligations Brought Forward, October 1	$ 40,548	$ 5,926	$ 43,814	$ 13,158
Obligations Incurred	779	14,100	27,555	8,248
Gross Outlays	(4,675)	(14,092)	(30,675)	(9,366)
Recoveries of Prior-Year Unpaid Obligations	(7,246)	(4,941)	(146)	(6,114)
Unpaid Obligations, End of Year	29,406	993	40,548	5,926
Uncollected Payments from Federal Sources:				
Uncollected Payments Brought Forward, October 1	$ -	$ (349)	$ -	$ (496)
Change in Uncollected Payments	-	123	-	147
Uncollected Payments from Federal Sources, End of Year	-	(226)	-	(349)
Obligated Balance, Net, End of Year	**$ 29,406**	**$ 767**	**$ 40,548**	**$ 5,577**
OBLIGATED BALANCES				
(Net of Unpaid Obligations and Uncollected Payments Above)				
Obligated Balance, Net, Brought Forward, October 1	**$ 40,548**	**$ 5,577**	**$ 43,814**	**$ 12,662**
Obligated Balance, Net, End of Year	**$ 29,406**	**$ 767**	**$ 40,548**	**$ 5,577**
BUDGET AUTHORITY AND OUTLAYS, NET				
Budget Authority, Gross	$ 789	$ 13,339	$ 27,593	$ 24,354
Actual Offsetting Collections	(1)	(36,604)	-	(81,269)
Change in Uncollected Customer Payments from Federal Sources	-	123	-	147
BUDGET AUTHORITY, NET	**$ 788**	**$ (23,142)**	**$ 27,593**	**$ (56,768)**
Gross Outlays	$ 4,675	$ 14,092	$ 30,675	$ 9,366
Actual Offsetting Collections	(1)	(36,604)	-	(81,269)
Net Outlays	4,674	(22,512)	30,675	(71,903)
Distributed Offsetting Receipts	(13,218)	-	(6,063)	-
AGENCY OUTLAYS, NET	**$ (8,544)**	**$ (22,512)**	**$ 24,612**	**$ (71,903)**

The accompanying notes are an integral part of these financial statements.

NOTES TO THE FINANCIAL STATEMENTS

NOTE 1. REPORTING ENTITY

The Troubled Asset Relief Program (TARP) was authorized by the Emergency Economic Stabilization Act of 2008, as amended (EESA or "the Act"). The Act gave the Secretary of the Treasury (the Secretary) broad and flexible authority to establish the TARP to purchase and insure mortgages and other troubled assets, which permitted the Secretary to inject capital into banks and other commercial companies by taking equity positions in those entities to help stabilize the financial markets.

The EESA established certain criteria under which the TARP would operate, including provisions that impact the budgeting, accounting, and reporting of troubled assets acquired under the Act. Section 115 of the EESA limited the authority of the Secretary to purchase troubled assets up to $700.0 billion outstanding at any one time, calculated as the aggregate purchase prices of all troubled assets held. In July 2010, the Dodd-Frank Wall Street Reform and Consumer Protection Act amended Section 115 of the EESA, limiting the TARP's authority to a total of $475.0 billion cumulative obligations (i.e. purchases and guarantees) and prohibiting any new obligations for programs or initiatives that had not been publicly announced prior to June 25, 2010. Of the maximum $475.0 billion authority under the EESA, OFS had utilized (including purchases made, legal commitments to make purchases and offsets for guarantees made) $456.6 billion as of September 30, 2013 and $467.0 billion as of September 30, 2012. The reduction between 2013 and 2012 reflects the deobligation of unused funds in certain programs.

The TARP developed the following programs: the Capital Purchase Program (CPP); the Community Development Capital Initiative (CDCI); the Public-Private Investment Program (PPIP); the Term Asset-Backed Securities Loan Facility (TALF); the SBA 7(a) Securities Purchase Program (SBA 7(a)); the Automotive Industry Financing Program (AIFP); the American International Group, Inc. (AIG) Investment Program (formerly known as the Systemically Significant Failing Institutions Program); the Asset

Guarantee Program (AGP); and the Treasury Housing Programs Under TARP (see Notes 5 and 6 for details regarding all of these programs).

While these financial statements reflect the activity of the OFS in executing its programs, including providing resources to various entities to help stabilize the financial markets, they do not include the assets, liabilities, or results of operations of commercial entities in which the OFS has a significant equity interest. Through the purchase of troubled assets, the OFS entered into several different types of direct loan, equity investment, and other credit programs (which consist of the AGP and the Federal Housing Administration (FHA) Refinance Program) (collectively, the OFS programs) with private entities. The OFS programs were entered into with the intent of helping to stabilize the financial markets and mitigating, as best as possible, any adverse impact on the economy; they were not entered into to engage in the business activities of the respective private entities. Based on this intent, the OFS concluded that such programs are considered "bailouts," under the provisions of paragraph 50 of Statement of Federal Financial Accounting Concepts (SFFAC) No. 2, *Entity and Display*. In addition, these entities are not included in the Federal budget and, therefore, do not meet the conclusive criteria in SFFAC No. 2. As such, the OFS determined that none of these entities should be classified as a federal entity. Consequently, their assets, liabilities and results of operations were not consolidated in these OFS financial statements, but the value of such investments was recorded in the OFS financial statements.

In addition, the OFS has made loans and investments in certain Special Purpose Vehicles (SPV)[4]. SFFAC No. 2, paragraphs 43 and 44,

---

[4] During fiscal year 2013, the OFS held investments in SPVs under the TALF and PPIP programs; in fiscal year 2012, the OFS held investments in SPVs under the TALF, PPIP and AIG Investment Programs.

reference indicative criteria such as ownership and control to carry out government powers and missions, as criteria in the determination about whether an entity should be classified as a federal entity. The OFS has concluded that none of the SPVs meet the conclusive or indicative criteria to be classified as a federal entity. As a result, the assets, liabilities and results of operations of the SPVs are not included in these OFS financial statements. Additional disclosures regarding certain SPV investments are included in Notes 2 and 6; see PPIP, TALF and AIG Investment Program.

The EESA established the OFS within the Office of Domestic Finance of the U. S. Department of the Treasury (Treasury) to administer the TARP and required its separate audited financial statements. The OFS prepares stand-alone financial statements for TARP to satisfy EESA Section 116(b)(1). Additionally, as an office of the Treasury, its financial statements are consolidated into Treasury's Agency Financial Report.

NOTE 2. SUMMARY OF SIGNIFICANT ACCOUNTING POLICIES

Basis of Accounting and Presentation

The accompanying financial statements include the results of operations of the TARP and have been prepared from the accounting records of the OFS in conformity with accounting principles generally accepted in the United States for federal entities (Federal GAAP), and the OMB Circular A-136, *Financial Reporting Requirements*, as amended. Federal GAAP includes the standards issued by the Federal Accounting Standards Advisory Board (FASAB). The FASAB is recognized by the American Institute of Certified Public Accountants (AICPA) as the official accounting standards-setting body for the U.S. Government.

Section 123(a) of the EESA requires that the budgetary cost of purchases of troubled assets and guarantees of troubled assets, and any cash flows associated with authorized activities, be determined in accordance with the Federal Credit Reform Act of 1990 (FCRA). Section 123(b) (1) of the EESA requires that the budgetary costs of troubled assets and guarantees of troubled assets be calculated by adjusting the discount rate for market risks. As a result of this requirement, the OFS considered market risk in its calculation and determination of the estimated net present value of its direct loans, equity investments and other credit programs for budgetary purposes. Similarly, market risk is considered in the valuations for financial reporting purposes (see Note 6 for further discussion).

Consistent with its accounting policy for equity investments in private entities, including SPVs, the OFS accounts for its equity investments at fair value. Since fair value is not defined in federal accounting standards as established in Statement of Federal Financial Accounting Standards (SFFAS) No. 34, *The Hierarchy of Generally Accepted Accounting Principles, Including the Application of Standards Issued by the Financial Accounting Standards Board*, the OFS conforms to fair value definitions contained in the private sector Financial Accounting Standards Codification (ASC) 820, *Fair Value Measurement*. OFS defines fair value of its equity investments as the estimated amount of

proceeds that would be received if the equity investments were sold to a market participant in an orderly transaction. Note 6 presents Direct Loan and Equity Investments and the Asset Guarantee Program receivable tabulated by the Level of Observation of the inputs used in the valuation process. Level 1 assets are measured using quoted market prices for identical assets. Level 2 assets are measured using observable market inputs other than direct market quotes. Level 3 assets are measured using unobservable inputs.

The OFS uses the present value accounting concepts embedded in SFFAS No. 2, *Accounting for Direct Loans and Loan Guarantees,* as amended (SFFAS No. 2), to derive fair value measurements for its equity investments in Levels 2 and 3. The OFS concluded that some of the equity investments, such as preferred stock, were similar to direct loans since there was a stated rate and a redemption feature which, if elected, required repayment of the amount invested. Furthermore, consideration of market risk provided a basis to arrive at a fair value measurement. Therefore, the OFS concluded that SFFAS No. 2 (as more fully discussed below) should be followed for reporting and disclosure requirements of its equity investments.

The OFS applies the provisions of FCRA for budgetary accounting and the associated FASAB accounting standard SFFAS No. 2 for financial reporting for direct loans and other credit programs. Direct loans disbursed and outstanding are recognized as assets at the net present value of their estimated future cash flows. Outstanding asset guarantees are recognized as liabilities or assets at the net present value of their estimated future cash flows. Liabilities under the FHA-Refinance Program are recognized at the net present value of their estimated future cash flows when the FHA guarantees loans.

For direct loans and equity investments, the subsidy allowance account represents the difference between the face value of the outstanding direct loan and equity investment balance and the net present value of the expected future cash flows or fair value, and is reported as an adjustment to the face value of the direct loan or equity investment.

The OFS recognizes dividend income associated with equity investments when declared by the entity in which the OFS has invested and when received in relation to any repurchases, exchanges and restructurings. The OFS recognizes interest income when earned on performing loans; interest income is not accrued on non-performing loans. The OFS reflects changes, referred to as reestimates, in its determination of the value of direct loans, equity investments, and other credit programs in the subsidy cost on the Statement of Net Cost annually.

In certain programs, the OFS has received common stock warrants, additional preferred stock (referred to as warrant preferred stock) or additional notes as additional consideration. The OFS accounts for any proceeds received from the sale of these investments as fees under SFFAS No. 2; as such, they are credited to the subsidy allowance rather than to income.

Use of Estimates

The OFS has made certain estimates and assumptions relating to the reporting of assets, liabilities, revenues, and cost to prepare these financial statements. Actual results could significantly differ from these estimates. Major financial statement lines that include estimates are Direct Loans and Equity Investments, Net, the Asset Guarantee Program and the Liabilities for Treasury Housing Programs Under TARP on the Balance Sheet, and related Program Subsidy Cost (Income) on the Statement of Net Cost (see Note 6).

The most significant differences between actual results and estimates may occur in the valuation of OFS programs. These valuation estimates are sensitive to slight changes in model assumptions, such as general economic conditions, specific stock price volatility of the entities in which the OFS has an equity interest, estimates of expected default, and prepayment rates. Forecasts of future financial results have inherent uncertainty, and the Direct Loans and Equity Investments, Net and Asset Guarantee Program line items, as of fiscal year ends, primarily reflect relatively illiquid assets with values that are sensitive to future economic conditions and other assumptions. Estimates are also prepared for the FHA-Refinance Program to determine the liability for losses.

Credit Reform Accounting

The OFS accounts for the cost of direct loans, equity investments and other credit programs in accordance with Section 123(a) of the EESA and the FCRA for budgetary accounting, and fair value and SFFAS No. 2 for financial reporting. The FCRA calls for the establishment of program, financing and general fund receipt accounts to segregate and report receipts and disbursements. These accounts are classified as either budgetary or non-budgetary in the Statement of Budgetary Resources. The OFS maintains budgetary program accounts which receive appropriations and obligate funds to cover the subsidy cost of direct loans, equity investments and other credit programs, and disburses the subsidy cost to the OFS financing accounts. The financing accounts are non-budgetary accounts that are used to record all of the cash flows resulting from the OFS direct loans, equity investments and other credit programs. Cash flows include disbursements, borrower repayments, repurchases, fees, recoveries, interest, dividends, proceeds from the sale of stock and warrants, borrowings from and repayments to Treasury, negative subsidy and the subsidy cost received from the program accounts, as well as subsidy reestimates and modifications.

Financing arrangements specifically for the TARP activities are provided for in EESA as follows: (1) borrowing for program funds under Section 118, reported as "appropriations" in these financial statements and (2) borrowing by financing accounts for amounts not covered by subsidy cost, under the FCRA and Section 123. The OFS uses budgetary general fund receipt accounts to record the receipt of amounts paid from the financing accounts when there is a negative subsidy or negative modification (a reduction in subsidy cost due to changes in program policy or terms that change estimated future cash flows) from the original estimate or a downward reestimate. Any assets in these accounts are non-entity assets, not available to the OFS, and are offset by intragovernmental liabilities. At the end of the fiscal year, the fund balance transferred to the U.S. Treasury through the general fund receipt accounts is not included in the OFS's reported Fund Balance with Treasury.

SFFAS No. 2 requires that the actual and expected costs of federal credit programs be fully recognized in financial reporting. The OFS calculated and recorded initial estimates of the future performance of direct loans, equity investments, and other credit programs. The data used for these estimates were reestimated annually, at fiscal year end, to reflect adjustments for market risk, asset performance, and other key variables and economic factors. The reestimate data were then used to estimate and report the "Program Subsidy Cost (Income)" in the Statement of Net Cost. A detailed discussion of the OFS subsidy calculation and reestimate assumptions, process and results is provided in Note 6.

Fund Balance with Treasury

The Fund Balance with Treasury includes general, financing and other funds available to pay current liabilities and finance authorized purchases. Cash receipts and disbursements are processed by the Treasury, and the OFS's records are reconciled with those of the Treasury on a regular basis.

Available unobligated balances represent amounts that are apportioned for obligation in the current fiscal year. Unavailable unobligated balances represent unanticipated collections in excess of the amounts apportioned which are unavailable. Obligated balances not yet disbursed include undelivered orders and unpaid expended authority. See Note 3.

Direct Loans and Equity Investments, Net

Direct Loans and Equity Investments, Net represents the estimated net outstanding amount of the OFS direct loans and equity investments. The direct loan and equity investment balances have been determined in accordance with the provisions of SFFAS No. 2 or at fair value (see Note 6). Write-offs of gross direct loan and equity investment balances (presented in Note 6 table) are recorded when a legal event occurs, such as a bankruptcy with no further chance of recovery or extinguishment of a debt instrument by agreement. Under SFFAS No. 2, write-offs do not affect the Statement of Net Cost because the written-off asset is fully reserved. Therefore, the write-off removes the asset balance and the associated subsidy allowance.

Asset Guarantee Program

During fiscal year 2010, the OFS and the Federal Deposit Insurance Corporation (FDIC) entered into a termination agreement with the Asset Guarantee Program's sole participant, Citigroup. As a result, the Intragovernmental Asset line item, Asset Guarantee Program, remaining on the Balance Sheet at September 30, 2012 was the estimated value of certain Citigroup trust preferred securities including dividends collected, held by the FDIC for the benefit of OFS. Under the termination agreement, the FDIC transferred those securities to the OFS, less any losses on FDIC's guarantee of Citigroup debt, in fiscal year 2013. OFS then sold the securities. See Note 6.

General Property and Equipment

Equipment with a cost of $50,000 or more per unit and a useful life of two years or more is capitalized at full cost and depreciated using the straight-line method over the equipment's useful life. Other equipment not meeting the capitalization criteria is expensed when purchased. Software developed for internal use is capitalized and amortized over the estimated useful life of the software if the cost per project is greater than $250,000. However, OFS may expense such software if management concludes that total period costs would not be materially distorted and the cost of capitalization is not economically prudent. Based upon these criteria, the OFS reports no capitalized property, equipment or software on its Balance Sheet as of September 30, 2013 and 2012.

Accounts Payable and Other Liabilities

Accounts Payable and Other Liabilities are amounts due to intragovernmental or public entities that are anticipated to be liquidated during the next operating cycle (within one year from the balance sheet date).

Due to the General Fund

Due to the General Fund represents the amount of accrued downward reestimates not yet funded, related to direct loans, equity investments and other credit programs as of September 30, 2013 and 2012. See Notes 6 and 7.

Principal Payable to the Bureau of the Fiscal Service

Principal Payable to the Bureau of the Fiscal Service (Fiscal Service)(formerly Principal Payable to the Bureau of Public Debt; the Department of the Treasury combined the functions of the Bureau of Public Debt and the Financial Management Service into the Fiscal Service on October 7, 2012) is the net amount due for equity investments, direct loans and other credit programs funded by borrowings from the Fiscal Service as of the end of the fiscal year. Additionally, OFS borrows from the Fiscal Service for payment of intragovernmental interest and payment of negative subsidy cost to the general fund, as necessary. See Note 8.

Liabilities for the Treasury Housing Programs Under TARP

There are three initiatives in the Treasury Housing Programs: the Making Home Affordable Program, the Housing Finance Agency Hardest-Hit Fund and the FHA-Refinance Program. The OFS has determined that credit reform accounting is not applicable to the Treasury Housing Programs Under TARP except for the FHA-Refinance Program. Therefore, liabilities for the Making Home Affordable Program and Housing Finance Agency Hardest-Hit Fund are accounted for in accordance with SFFAS No. 5, *Accounting for Liabilities of the Federal Government*. In accordance with this standard, a liability is recognized for any unpaid amounts due and payable as of the reporting date. The liability estimate, as of September 30, 2013 and 2012, is based on information about loan modifications reported by participating servicers for the Making Home Affordable Program and participating states for the Housing Finance Agency Hardest-Hit Fund. See Note 5.

At the end of fiscal year 2010, the OFS entered into a loss-sharing agreement with the FHA to support a program in which FHA would guarantee refinancing for borrowers whose homes are worth less than the remaining amounts owed under their mortgage loans, i.e. "underwater." The liability for OFS's share of losses was determined under credit reform accounting and shown as FHA-Refinance Program,

one of the Liabilities for Treasury Housing Programs Under TARP, on the Balance Sheet. See Notes 4, 5 and 6.

Unexpended Appropriations

Unexpended Appropriations represents the OFS undelivered orders and unobligated balances in budgetary appropriated funds as of September 30, 2013 and 2012.

Cumulative Results of Operations

Cumulative Results of Operations, presented on the Balance Sheet and on the Statement of Changes in Net Position, represents the net results of the OFS operations not funded by appropriations or some other source, such as borrowing authority, from inception through fiscal year end. At September 30, 2012, OFS had $755 million of unfunded upward reestimates that resulted in OFS reporting negative Cumulative Results of Operations. These unfunded upward reestimates were funded in fiscal year 2013. Cumulative Results of Operations in 2013 and 2012 also included $50 million reported as Cash on Deposit for Housing Program on the Balance Sheet, see Note 4.

Other Financing Sources

The Other Financing Sources line in the Statement of Changes in Net Position for each year consists primarily of downward reestimates. Each program's reestimates, upward and downward, are recorded separately, not netted together.

Leave

A liability for the OFS employees' annual leave is accrued as it is earned and reduced as leave is taken. Each year the balance of accrued annual leave is adjusted to reflect current pay rates as well as forfeited "use or lose" leave. Amounts are unfunded to the extent current or prior year appropriations are not available to fund annual leave earned but not taken. Sick leave and other types of non-vested leave are expensed as taken. The liability is included in the Balance Sheet amount for Accounts Payable and Other Liabilities.

Employee Health and Life Insurance and Workers' Compensation Benefits

The OFS employees may choose to participate in the contributory Federal Employees Health Benefit and the Federal Employees Group Life Insurance Programs. The OFS matches a portion of the employee contributions to each program. Matching contributions are recognized as current operating expenses.

The Federal Employees' Compensation Act (FECA) provides income and medical cost protection to covered Federal civilian employees injured on the job, and employees who have incurred a work-related injury or occupational disease. Future workers' compensation estimates are generated from an application of actuarial procedures developed to estimate the liability for FECA benefits. The actuarial liability estimates for FECA benefits include the expected liability for death, disability, medical, and miscellaneous costs for approved compensation cases. Any FECA amounts relating to OFS employees are expensed as incurred.

Employee Pension Benefits

The OFS employees participate in either the Civil Service Retirement System (CSRS) or the Federal Employees' Retirement System (FERS) and Social Security. These systems provide benefits upon retirement and in the event of death, disability or other termination of employment and may also provide pre-retirement benefits. They may also include benefits to survivors and their dependents, and may contain early retirement or other special features. The OFS contributions to retirement plans and Social Security, as well as imputed costs for pension and other retirement benefit costs administered by the Office of Personnel Management, are recognized on the Statement of Net Cost as Administrative Cost. Federal employee benefits also include the Thrift Savings Plan (TSP). For FERS employees, a TSP account is automatically established and the OFS matches employee contributions to the plan, subject to limitations. The matching contributions are recognized as Administrative Costs on the Statement of Net Cost.

Related Parties

The nature of related parties and descriptions of related party transactions are discussed within Notes 1 and 6.

NOTE 3. FUND BALANCES WITH TREASURY

Fund Balances with Treasury, by fund type and status, as of September 30, 2013 and 2012, are presented in the following table.

(Dollars in Millions)	As of September 30,	
	2013	2012
Fund Balances:		
General Funds	$ 36,630	$ 40,517
Program Funds	14,382	14,382
Financing Funds	2,228	20,596
Total Fund Balances	$ 53,240	$ 75,495
Status of Fund Balances:		
Unobligated Balances		
Available	678	3,987
Unavailable	22,389	27,994
Obligated Balances Not Yet Disbursed	30,173	43,514
Total Status of Fund Balances	$ 53,240	$ 75,495

Collections relating to the AGP are deposited in the Troubled Assets Insurance Financing Fund (which is within OFS Financing Funds balance) as required by the EESA Section 102(d). In fiscal year 2013 the TAIFF was closed because the AGP program was completed and investments sold. In fiscal year 2012 the TAIFF balance was reduced for AGP-related downward reestimates, repayments of AGP-related debt and interest payments on debt due to the Bureau of the Public Debt.

NOTE 4. CASH ON DEPOSIT FOR HOUSING PROGRAM

As of September 30, 2013 and 2012, the OFS had $50 million on deposit with a commercial bank to facilitate its payments of claims under the FHA-Refinance Program as OFS's agent.

Under terms of the agreement with the commercial bank, unused funds will be returned to the OFS upon the termination of the program.

NOTE 5. TREASURY HOUSING PROGRAMS UNDER TARP

Fiscal years 2013 and 2012 saw continued advancement of programs designed to provide stability for both the housing market and homeowners. These programs assist homeowners who are experiencing financial hardships to remain in their homes until their financial position improves or they relocate to a more sustainable living situation. The programs fall into three initiatives:

1) Making Home Affordable Program (MHA);
2) Hardest-Hit Fund (HHF); and
3) FHA-Refinance Program.

Features of these initiatives follow:

Housing Program	Features
MHA	
Home Affordable Modification Program (HAMP)	
First Lien Modification Program	Provides for upfront, monthly and annual incentives to servicers, borrowers and investors who participate, whereby the investor and OFS share the costs of modifying qualified first liens, conditional on borrower performance.
Principal Reduction Alternative Program (PRA)	Pays financial incentives to investors for principal reduction in conjunction with a first lien HAMP modification.
Home Price Depreciation Program (HPDP)	Provides financial incentives to investors to partially offset losses from home price declines.
Home Affordable Foreclosure Alternatives (HAFA)	Designed to assist eligible borrowers unable to retain their homes through a HAMP modification, by simplifying and streamlining the short sale and deed-in-lieu of foreclosure processes and providing financial incentives to servicers and investors as well as relocation assistance to borrowers who pursue short sales and deeds-in-lieu.
Unemployment Forebearance Program (UP)	Offers assistance to unemployed homeowners through temporary forebearance of a portion of their mortgage payments. This program does not require any payments from OFS.
FHA-HAMP	Provides mortgage modifications similar to HAMP, but for FHA-insured or guaranteed loans offered by the FHA, VA or USDA.
Second Lien Program (2MP)	Offers financial incentives to participating servicers who modify second liens in conjunction with a HAMP modification.
Treasury/FHA Second Lien Program (FHA 2LP)	Provides for reduction or elimination of second mortgages on homes whose servicers participate in the FHA Refinance Program.
Rural Development Program (RD-HAMP)	Provides for lower monthly payments on USDA guaranteed loans.
HHF	Provides targeted aid to homeowners in the states hardest hit by the housing market downturn and unemployment.
FHA-Refinance Program	Joint initiative with HUD to encourage refinancing of existing underwater mortgage loans not currently insured by FHA into FHA insured mortgages.

MHA

In early 2009, Treasury launched the Making Home Affordable Program (MHA) to help struggling homeowners avoid foreclosure. Since its inception, MHA has helped homeowners avoid foreclosure by providing a variety of solutions to modify or refinance their mortgages, get temporary forbearance if they are unemployed, or transition out of homeownership via a short sale or deed-in-lieu of foreclosure. The cornerstone of MHA is the Home Affordable Modification Program (HAMP), which provides eligible homeowners the opportunity to reduce their monthly mortgage payments to more affordable levels. Treasury also launched programs under MHA to help homeowners who are unemployed, "underwater" on their loans (those who owe more on their home than it is currently worth), or struggling with second liens. It also includes options for homeowners who would like to transition to a more affordable living situation through a short sale or deed-in-lieu of foreclosure. MHA includes several additional programs to help homeowners refinance or address specific types of mortgages, in conjunction with the Federal Housing Administration (FHA), the U. S. Department of Agriculture (USDA), and the U. S. Department of Veterans Affairs (VA).

In fiscal year 2013, the deadline for applications under the MHA programs was extended from December 31, 2013, to December 31, 2015.

In fiscal year 2012, the OFS made additional changes to MHA programs to provide relief to more homeowners and accelerate the housing market recovery. HAMP program guidelines were expanded through the introduction of a second-level evaluation that expands the population of homeowners eligible for the programs, including certain rental properties and vacancies, creating a flexible debt-to-income ratio band and including certain previous HAMP participants who may have lost good standing. Finally, investor incentives for PRA were tripled on first liens and doubled on second liens, and servicer incentives were restructured to promote early engagement with the borrowers.

All MHA disbursements are made to servicers either for themselves or for the benefit of borrowers and investors, and all payments are contingent on borrowers remaining in good standing.

Fannie Mae, as the MHA Program Administrator, provides direct programmatic support as a third party agent on behalf of the OFS. Freddie Mac provides compliance oversight of servicers as a third party agent on behalf of the OFS, and the servicers work directly with the borrowers to modify and service the borrowers' loans. Fees paid to Fannie Mae and Freddie Mac are included in administrative costs reported on the Statement of Net Cost.

HHF

The HHF was implemented in fiscal year 2010, and provides targeted aid to homeowners in the states hit hardest by the housing market downturn and unemployment through each state's Housing Finance Agency (HFA). States that meet the criteria for this program consist of Alabama, Arizona, California, Florida, Georgia, Illinois, Indiana, Kentucky, Michigan, Mississippi, Nevada, New Jersey, North Carolina, Ohio, Oregon, Rhode Island, South Carolina, Tennessee, as well as the District of Columbia. Approved states develop and roll out their own programs with timing and types of programs offered targeted to address the specific needs and economic conditions of their state. States have until December 31, 2017 to enter into agreements with borrowers.

In fiscal year 2013, the state HFAs continued to adapt their programs to best meet borrower needs in evolving economic and housing markets. A total of seven HFAs now offer principal reduction to enable a loan modification, refinance, or recast, and other states are strongly considering this model. Florida, Illinois and Ohio have utilized HHF resources to purchase notes and modify the underlying loan terms, and Oregon offers refinancing options to underwater homeowners ineligible for other options. Additionally, Michigan has elected to designate a portion of its HHF allocation for blight elimination activities that target vacant and abandoned urban residences. Ohio has submitted a proposal to do the same, and other states are contemplating this approach to foreclosure prevention.

In fiscal year 2012, the state HFAs made substantial eligibility changes to existing programs (e.g. Florida, New Jersey) and significantly modified principal reduction programs (e.g. Arizona, California and Nevada) incorporating curtailments (i.e. unmatched principal reduction) that can be applied to all eligible loans including GSE loans that historically have not participated in principal reduction programs.

FHA-Refinance Program

The FHA-Refinance Program is a joint initiative with the U. S. Department of Housing and Urban Development (HUD) which is intended to encourage refinancing of existing underwater mortgage loans not currently insured by FHA into FHA-insured mortgages. HUD will pay a portion of the amount refinanced to the investor and OFS will pay incentives to encourage the extinguishment of second liens associated with the refinanced mortgages. OFS established a letter of credit that obligated the OFS portion of any claims associated with the FHA-guaranteed mortgages. The OMB determined that for budgetary purposes, the FHA-Refinance Program cost is calculated under the FCRA, and accordingly OFS determined that it was appropriate to follow SFFAS No. 2 for financial reporting. Therefore, the liability is calculated at the net present value of estimated future cash flows. Homeowners can refinance into FHA-guaranteed mortgages through December 31, 2014, and OFS will honor its share of claims against the letter of credit through September 2020. As of September 30, 2013, 3,015 loans had been refinanced. As of September 30, 2012, 1,774 loans had been refinanced.

OFS deposited $50 million with a commercial bank as its agent to administer payment of claims under the program; $47,840 in claim payments were made as of September 30, 2013. No claim payments had been made as of September 30, 2012. See Notes 4 and 6 for further details about the deposit and the program. OFS paid $2 million each year in fiscal years 2013 and 2012 to maintain the letter of credit.

The table below recaps housing program total commitments as of September 30, 2013, and payments and accruals as of September 30, 2013 and 2012.

Treasury Housing Programs Under TARP

(Dollars in Millions)	Total Commitments as of September 30, 2013[1]	Fiscal Year Payments through September 30,		Accruals as of September 30,	
		2013	2012	2013	2012
MHA	$ 29,867	$ 2,541	$ 2,202	$ 263	$ 241
HFA Hardest Hit Fund	7,600	1,396	861	-	-
FHA - Refinance[2]	1,025	2	2	-	-
Totals	$ 38,492	$ 3,939	$ 3,065	$ 263	$ 241

[1] Total commitments represent amounts obligated to support all of OFS's Housing programs. This differs from the $28,747 outstanding commitments as of September 30, 2013, which are the remaining funds available to be spent.

[2] Payments do not include $50 million to establish reserve, shown on Balance Sheet as Cash on Deposit for Housing Program, nor the subsidy cost to fund OFS's estimated share of defaults, which establishes the liability for losses, see Note 6. Payments are the FHA-Refinance administrative expense only.

NOTE 6. TROUBLED ASSET RELIEF PROGRAM DIRECT LOANS AND EQUITY INVESTMENTS, NET AND OTHER CREDIT PROGRAMS

The OFS administers a number of programs designed to help stabilize the financial system and restore the flow of credit to consumers and businesses. The OFS made direct loans and equity investments under TARP. The OFS also entered into other credit programs, which consist of an asset guarantee program and a loss-sharing program under the TARP. The table below recaps OFS programs by title and type:

	Program Type
Direct Loans and Equity Investments	
Capital Purchase Program	Equity Investment/Subordinated Debentures
Community Development Capital Initiative	Equity Investment/Subordinated Debentures
Public-Private Investment Program	Equity Investment and Direct Loan
Term Asset-Backed Securities Loan Facility	Subordinated Debentures
SBA 7(a) Security Purchase Program	Direct Loan
Automotive Industry Financing Program	Equity Investment and Direct Loan
American International Group, Inc. Investment Program	Equity Investment
Other Credit Programs	
Asset Guarantee Program	Asset Guarantee
FHA-Refinance Program	Loss-sharing Program with FHA

Direct Loan and Equity Investment Programs

Capital Purchase Program (CPP)

In October 2008, the OFS began implementation of the TARP with the Capital Purchase Program (CPP), designed to help stabilize the financial system by assisting in building the capital base of certain viable U.S. financial institutions to increase the capacity of those institutions to lend to businesses and consumers and support the economy.

The OFS invested a total of $204.9 billion in 707 institutions under the CPP program between October 2008 and December 2009.

Under this program, the OFS purchased senior perpetual preferred stock from qualifying U.S. controlled banks, savings associations, and certain bank and savings and loan holding companies (Qualified Financial Institution or QFI). The senior preferred stock has a stated dividend rate of 5.0 percent through year five, increasing to 9.0 percent in subsequent years. The dividends are cumulative for bank holding companies and non-cumulative for others; they are payable when and if declared by the institution's board of directors. In addition to the senior preferred stock, the OFS received warrants, with a 10-year term, as required by section 113(d) of EESA, from public QFIs to purchase a number of shares of common stock. QFIs that are Subchapter S corporations issued subordinated debentures instead of preferred stock (to comply with tax code regulations) with interest rates of 7.7 percent for the first five years and 13.8 percent thereafter.

The OFS received warrants from non-public QFIs for the purchase of additional senior preferred stock (or subordinated debentures if appropriate) with a stated dividend rate of 9.0 percent (13.8 percent interest rate for subordinate debentures) and a liquidation preference equal to 5.0 percent of the total senior preferred stock (additional subordinate debenture) investment. These warrants were immediately exercised and resulted in the OFS holding additional senior preferred stock (subordinated debentures) (collectively referred to as "warrant preferred stock") of non-public QFIs.

In addition to the above transactions, the OFS entered into other transactions with various financial institutions including exchanging existing preferred shares for a like amount of non-tax-deductible Trust Preferred Securities, exchanging preferred shares for shares of mandatorily convertible preferred securities and selling preferred shares to financial institutions that were acquiring the QFIs that have issued the preferred shares. Generally, these transactions are entered into with financial institutions in poor financial condition with a high likelihood of failure. As such, in accordance with SFFAS 2, these transactions are considered workouts and not modifications. The changes in cost associated with these transactions are captured in the year-end reestimates.

During fiscal year 2012, OFS elected to sell selected CPP investments to the public in auction sales. Because auction sales were not considered in the budget formulation estimate for the CPP program, OFS recorded a modification increasing the cost of the program by $973 million. During fiscal year 2013, OFS continued auction sales of selected remaining CPP investments.

In fiscal year 2013, OFS sold 113 CPP investments in 14 separate auctions for total net proceeds of $1.5 billion. These auction sales resulted in net proceeds less than cost of $455 million. In addition, other sales and redemptions for 60 institutions resulted in net proceeds less than cost of $38 million.

In fiscal year 2012, OFS sold 40 CPP investments in six separate auctions for total net proceeds of $1.3 billion. These auction sales resulted in net proceeds less than cost of $180 million. In addition, other sales and redemptions for 56 institutions resulted in net proceeds less than cost of $105 million.

During fiscal year 2013, one CPP institution was written off for $104 million. OFS originally invested $110 million and recovered $6 million. There were no write-offs in fiscal year 2012. During fiscal year 2013, seven institutions, in which OFS had invested $137 million, were either closed by their regulators or declared bankruptcy. During fiscal year 2012, six institutions, in which OFS had invested $51 million, were either closed by their regulators or declared bankruptcy. The OFS does not anticipate recovery on these investments and therefore the values of these investments are reflected at zero as of September 30, 2013 and 2012. The ultimate amount received, if any, from the investments in institutions that filed for bankruptcy and institutions closed by regulators will depend primarily on the outcome of the bankruptcy proceedings and of each institution's receivership.

The following tables provide key data points related to the CPP for the fiscal years ending September 30, 2013 and 2012:

CPP Participating Institutions

	Cumulative as of September 30,	
	2013	2012
Number of Institutions Funded	707	707
Institutions Paid in Full, Merged or Investments Sold	(407)	(234)
Institutions Transferred to CDCI	(28)	(28)
Institutions Refinanced to SBLF	(137)	(137)
Institutions Written Off After Bankruptcy or Receivership	(3)	(2)
Number of Institutions with Outstanding OFS Investments	132	306
Institutions in Bankruptcy or Receivership	(24)	(17)
Number of CPP Institutions Valued at Year-End	**108**	**289**
Of the Institutions Valued, Number that Have Missed One or More Dividend Payments	76	157

CPP Investments

(Dollars in Millions)	Fiscal Year 2013	Fiscal Year 2012
Outstanding Beginning Balance, Investment in CPP Institutions, Gross	$ 8,664	$ 17,299
Repayments and Sales of Investments	(4,752)	(8,223)
Write-Offs	(104)	-
Losses from Sales and Repurchases of Assets in Excess of Cost	(665)	(412)
Outstanding Balance, Investment in CPP Institutions, Gross	**$ 3,143**	**$ 8,664**
Interest and Dividend Collections	$ 262	$ 572
Net Proceeds from Sales and Repurchases of Assets Less Than Cost	$ (493)	$ (285)

Community Development Capital Initiative (CDCI)

In February 2010, the OFS announced the Community Development Capital Initiative (CDCI) to invest lower cost capital in Community Development Financial Institutions (CDFIs). Under the terms of the program, the OFS purchased senior preferred stock (or subordinated debt) from eligible CDFIs. The senior preferred stock had an initial dividend rate of 2 percent. CDFIs could apply to receive capital up to 5 percent of risk-weighted assets. To encourage repayment while recognizing the unique circumstances facing CDFIs, the dividend rate increases to 9 percent after eight years.

For CDFI credit unions, the OFS purchased subordinated debt at rates equivalent to those offered to CDFIs and with similar terms. These institutions could apply for up to 3.5 percent of total assets - an amount approximately equivalent to the 5 percent of risk-weighted assets available to banks and thrifts.

CDFIs participating in the CPP, subject to certain criteria, were eligible to exchange, through September 30, 2010, their CPP preferred shares (subordinated debt) then held by OFS for CDCI preferred shares (subordinated debt). These exchanges were treated as disbursements from CDCI and repayments to CPP. OFS invested a total of $570 million ($363 million as a result of exchanges from CPP) in 84 institutions under the CDCI.

During fiscal year 2013, one CDCI institution, in which the OFS invested $7 million, was written off; there were no write-offs in fiscal year 2012. During fiscal year 2012, this CDCI institution was closed by its regulator. The OFS did not anticipate recovery on the investment and therefore its value was reflected at zero as of September 30, 2012.

In fiscal year 2013, OFS received $86 million in repayments and $11 million in dividends and interest from its CDCI investments. In fiscal year 2012, OFS received $3 million in repayments and $11 million in dividends and interest from its CDCI investments.

Public-Private Investment Program (PPIP)

The PPIP was part of the OFS's efforts to help restart the financial securities market and provide liquidity for legacy securities. Under this program, the OFS (as a limited partner) made equity investments in and loans to nine investment vehicles (referred to as Public Private Investment Funds or "PPIFs") established by private investment managers between September and December 2009. The OFS equity investments were used to match private capital and equaled 49.9 percent of the total equity invested. Each PPIF elected to receive a loan commitment equal to 100 percent of partnership equity. Agreements between the OFS and the PPIFs require cash flows from purchased securities received by the PPIFs to be distributed in accordance with a priority of payments schedule (waterfall) designed to help protect the interests of secured parties. Security cash flows collected are disbursed: 1) to pay administrative expenses; 2) to pay margin interest on permitted hedges; 3) to pay current period interest to OFS; 4) to maintain a required interest reserve account; 5) to pay principal on the OFS loan when the minimum Asset Coverage Ratio Test is not satisfied; 6) to pay other amounts on interest rate hedges if not paid under step 2 ; 7) for additional temporary investments or to prepay loans (both at the discretion of the PPIF); 8) for distributions to equity partners up to the lesser of 12 months' net interest collected or 8 percent of the funded capital commitments; 9) for loan prepayments to OFS; and 10) for distribution to equity partners.

As a condition of its investment, the OFS also received a warrant from each of the PPIFs entitling the OFS to 2.5 percent of investment proceeds (excluding those from temporary investments) otherwise allocable to the non-OFS partners after the PPIFs return of 100 percent of the non-OFS partners' capital contributions. Distributions relating to the warrants generally occur upon the final distribution of each partnership.

The PPIFs were allowed to purchase commercial and non-agency residential mortgage-backed securities (CMBS and RMBS, respectively) issued prior to January 1, 2009, that were originally rated AAA or an equivalent rating by two or more nationally recognized statistical rating organizations without external credit enhancement and that are secured directly by the actual mortgage loans, leases or other assets (eligible assets) and not other securities. The PPIF's investment period ended December 2012 and as of June 30, 2013, all of the PPIF's securities portfolios were completely liquidated. As of September 30, 2012, the PPIFs' portfolios were comprised of approximately 74 percent RMBS and 26 percent CMBS.

OFS made no disbursements to PPIFs during fiscal year 2013. During fiscal year 2012, OFS disbursed $245 million as equity investments and $803 million as loans to PPIFs.

In fiscal year 2013, the six remaining PPIFs liquidated investments and fully repaid investors, including OFS. During fiscal year 2013, the OFS received $17 million in interest on loans and $5.7 billion in loan principal repayments from the PPIFs and received $5.5 billion in equity distributions, of which $254 million was recognized as investment income, $1.2 billion as net proceeds in excess of cost and $4.1 billion as a reduction of the gross investment outstanding. During fiscal year 2012, the OFS received $124 million in interest on loans and $5.6 billion in loan principal repayments from the PPIFs and received $3.2 billion in equity distributions, of which $1.3 billion was recognized as investment income, $223 million as net proceeds in excess of cost and $1.7 billion as a reduction of the gross investment outstanding. One PPIF partnership fully repaid its investors, including OFS, in fiscal year 2012. Another had repaid all equity capital in fiscal year 2012 and distributed additional funds and ceased operations early in fiscal year 2013.

As of September 30, 2013, OFS had no PPIF equity investments or loans outstanding. The $10 million positive balance in the PPIP subsidy allowance account represents additional proceeds expected upon final liquidation of remaining partnerships. The legal commitments to disburse up to $1.8 billion in additional loans to remaining PPIFs as of September 30, 2012 were canceled in 2013 since all PPIFs had ceased operations. Commitments of $984 million to disburse additional equity to PPIFs will remain until all distributions have been received from PPIFs and all PPIF liabilities have been settled, although a requirement for additional disbursement by OFS is highly unlikely.

As of September 30, 2012, OFS had equity investments in six PPIFs outstanding of $4.1 billion and loans outstanding of $5.7 billion for a total of $9.8 billion. These investments and loans were valued at $10.8 billion.

Term Asset-Backed Securities Loan Facility (TALF)

The Term Asset-Backed Securities Loan Facility (TALF) was created by the Federal Reserve Board (FRB) to provide low cost funding to investors in certain classes of Asset-Backed Securities (ABS). The OFS agreed to participate in the program by providing liquidity and credit protection to the FRB.

Under the TALF, the Federal Reserve Bank of New York (FRBNY), as implementer of the TALF program, originated loans on a non-recourse basis to purchasers of certain AAA-rated ABS secured by consumer and commercial loans and commercial mortgage backed securities (CMBS). The FRBNY ceased issuing new loans on June 30, 2010. As of September 30, 2013, $101 million of loans due to the FRBNY remained outstanding. As of September 30, 2012, approximately $1.5 billion of loans due to the FRBNY remained outstanding.

As part of the program, the FRBNY created the TALF, LLC, a special purpose vehicle that agreed to purchase from the FRBNY any collateral it has seized due to borrower default. The TALF, LLC would fund purchases from the accumulation of monthly fees paid by the FRBNY as compensation for the agreement. Only if the TALF, LLC had insufficient funds to purchase the collateral did the OFS commit to invest up to $20.0 billion in non-recourse subordinated notes issued by the TALF, LLC. In July 2010, the OFS's commitment was reduced to $4.3 billion. In June 2012, the OFS's commitment was reduced from $4.3 billion to $1.4 billion. In fiscal year 2013, the remaining commitment was terminated.

The OFS disbursed $100 million upon the creation of TALF, LLC in 2009. Upon its wind-down, when collateral defaults, reaches final maturity or is sold, available cash will be disbursed to FRBNY and OFS according to the legal agreement between them.

In fiscal year 2013, a modification to the terms of the legal agreement resulted in $55 million in subsidy income for the program. The modification allowed

OFS to receive $100 million in repayments, $13 million in interest and $570 million of contingent interest, recorded as proceeds in excess of cost, in fiscal year 2013 rather than in fiscal year 2015 as originally expected.

As of September 30, 2013 and 2012, no TALF loans were in default and consequently no collateral was purchased by the TALF, LLC.

SBA 7(a) Securities Purchase Program

In March 2010, the OFS began the purchase of securities backed by Small Business Administration 7(a) loans (7(a) Securities) as part of the Unlocking Credit for Small Business Initiative. Under this program OFS purchased 7(a) Securities collateralized with 7(a) loans (these loans are guaranteed by the full faith and credit of the United States Government) packaged on or after July 1, 2008. In May 2011, OFS began selling its securities to investors. Sales were completed in January of 2012 and the program closed.

As of September 30, 2013 and 2012, the OFS held no investment in SBA 7(a) securities. The OFS invested a total of $367 million (excluding purchased accrued interest) and received $363 million in principal payments and sales proceeds, as well as $13 million in interest on its securities over the course of the program. During fiscal year 2012, the OFS sold its remaining SBA securities and received proceeds of $127 million, including interest.

Automotive Industry Financing Program (AIFP)

The Automotive Industry Financing Program (AIFP) was designed to help prevent a significant disruption of the American automotive industry, which could have had a negative effect on the economy of the United States.

General Motors Company (New GM) and General Motors Corporation (Old GM)

In the period ended September 30, 2009, the OFS provided $51.0 billion to General Motors Corporation (Old GM) through various loan agreements including the initial loan for general and working capital purposes, auto supplier and warranty programs, and the final loan for debtor-in-

possession (DIP) financing while Old GM was in bankruptcy. As of September 30, 2011, after various sales and restructurings of its investment, the OFS held 500 million shares of common stock of New GM, the post-bankruptcy GM entity, and had received a cumulative total of $23.9 billion in stock sale proceeds, loan repayments, dividends and interest.

During fiscal year 2013, OFS sold 399 million shares of GM common stock for $12.0 billion. The sales resulted in net proceeds less than cost of $5.4 billion. During fiscal year 2012, OFS did not sell any of its New GM common stock shares.

At September 30, 2013, the OFS held 101 million shares of the common stock of New GM that represented approximately 7.3 percent of the common stock of New GM outstanding. Market value of the 101 million shares as of September 30, 2013 was $3.6 billion. At September 30, 2012, the OFS held 500 million shares, approximately 32 percent of the common stock of New GM outstanding, with a market value of $11.4 billion.

In fiscal year 2011, $986 million of OFS's loan to Old GM was converted to an administrative claim. OFS retains the right to recover additional proceeds but recoveries are dependent on actual liquidation proceeds and pending litigation. OFS recovered $22 million and $26 million in fiscal years 2013 and 2012, respectively, on the administrative claim, and the outstanding balance at September 30, 2013 was $827 million. OFS does not expect to recover any significant additional proceeds from this claim.

Chrysler Group LLC (New Chrysler) and Chrysler Holding LLC (Old Chrysler)

During fiscal years 2009 and 2010, OFS invested $7.8 billion in Chrysler Holding LLC (Old Chrysler), including the auto supplier and warranty programs, and an additional $4.6 billion in Chrysler Group LLC (New Chrysler) under the terms of Chrysler's bankruptcy agreement. Prior to fiscal year 2012, pursuant to several agreements with New Chrysler that included writeoffs, OFS had received loan repayments, interest and additional payments totaling $11.1 billion and had no remaining interest in New Chrysler.

OFS continues to hold a right to receive proceeds from a bankruptcy liquidation trust related to Old Chrysler, but no significant cash flows are expected.

Nothing was received from the trust in fiscal year 2013; $9 million was received during fiscal year 2012. The underlying loan balance was extinguished in the Chrysler bankruptcy.

Ally Financial Inc. (formerly known as GMAC)

The OFS invested a total of $16.3 billion in GMAC between December 2008 and December 2009, to help support its ability to originate new loans to GM and Chrysler dealers and consumers and to help address GMAC's capital needs. In addition, in May 2009, under the terms of a separate $884 million loan to Old GM, OFS exercised its exchange option and received 190,921 shares of GMAC common stock from Old GM in full satisfaction of the loan. In May 2010, GMAC changed its corporate name to Ally Financial, Inc. (Ally), a private bank holding company. As a result of original investments, exchanges, conversions, warrant exercises and sales, at the beginning of fiscal year 2012, OFS had received $5.1 billion in sales proceeds and dividends on its initial investment and held 981,971 shares of common stock (73.8 percent of Ally's outstanding common stock) and 119 million shares of Series F-2 mandatorily convertible preferred securities (Series F-2). The Series F-2 were convertible into at least 513,000 shares of common stock.

Per an August 2013 agreement, all of the Series F-2 were repurchased by Ally from OFS for $5.2 billion in November 2013. OFS received an additional $725 million for the elimination of certain rights under the original agreement. This August 2013 agreement also included terms for Ally to issue a November 2013 private offering of new common stock at a price of $6,000 per share. Following this private offering, OFS's ownership was reduced to 63.4 percent of Ally's outstanding common stock. See the Valuation Methodology and Subsidy Cost and Reestimate sections of Note 6 for further discussion of the effects of this agreement.

The OFS received $534 million in dividends from the Ally investment each year in fiscal years 2013 and 2012.

The investment in Ally was valued at $12.0 billion at September 30, 2013, considering the effects of the August 2013 agreement: $5.9 billion for the common stock and $6.1 billion for the Series F-2.

At September 30, 2012, OFS's investment in Ally was valued at $6.2 billion based upon a model that calculated an average of three valuation benchmarks, since there was no direct market activity available.

American International Group, Inc. (AIG) Investment Program

The OFS provided assistance to systemically significant financial institutions on a case by case basis in order to help provide stability to institutions that were deemed critical to a functioning financial system and were at substantial risk of failure as well as to help prevent broader disruption to financial markets. OFS invested in one institution, AIG, under the program.

In November 2008, the OFS invested $40.0 billion in AIG in the form of Series D 10 percent cumulative perpetual preferred stock. An additional $27.8 billion was drawn from a capital facility made available to AIG by OFS, secured by additional preferred stock and common stock warrants. By January 2011, and as a result of various restructurings of both the OFS's and the Federal Reserve Bank of New York's investments in AIG, the OFS's entire investment outstanding consisted of $20.3 billion of interests in two AIG subsidiaries organized as Special Purpose Vehicles (the "AIG SPVs") and 1.1 billion shares of AIG common stock.

In fiscal year 2013, OFS sold the remainder of its common stock and warrants for $5.0 billion, resulting in proceeds less than cost of $1.7 billion. In fiscal year 2012, OFS received $9.6 billion in distributions from the AIG SPVs, paying off the remaining investment balance of $9.1 billion, recording proceeds in excess of cost of $127 million, and collecting $395 million of investment income (including $204 million capitalized and recognized as income in fiscal year 2011). OFS also sold 806 million shares of common stock for $25.2 billion. These proceeds were less than OFS's cost by $9.9 billion.

As of September 30, 2013, OFS retained no ownership interest in AIG, common or preferred, nor any interests in SPVs. At September 30, 2012, the OFS owned 154 million shares of AIG common stock, approximately 10.5 percent of AIG's common stock equity[5]. Market value of the common stock shares was $5.1 billion.

On its original $67.8 billion investment in AIG, OFS received $55.3 billion in repayments, sales proceeds, fees and dividends. OFS also incurred net interest cost of $2.7 billion, for a total subsidy cost of $15.2 billion, or 22.4 percent of its original investment.

Valuation Methodology

The OFS applies fair value and the provisions of SFFAS No. 2 to account for direct loans, equity investments and other credit programs. This standard requires measurement of the asset or liability at the net present value of the estimated future cash flows. The cash flow estimates for each transaction reflect the actual structure of the instruments. For each of these instruments, analytical cash flow models generate estimated cash flows to and from the OFS over the estimated term of the instrument. Further, each cash flow model reflects the specific terms and conditions of the program, technical assumptions regarding the underlying assets, risk of default or other losses, and other factors as appropriate. The models also incorporate an adjustment for market risk to reflect the additional return required by the market to compensate for variability around the expected losses reflected in the cash flows (the "unexpected loss").

The adjustment for market risk requires the OFS to determine the return that would be required by market participants to enter into similar transactions or to purchase the assets held by OFS. Accordingly, the measurement of the assets attempts to represent the proceeds expected to be received if the assets were sold to a market participant in an orderly transaction. The methodology employed for determining market risk for equity investments generally involves a calibration to market prices of similar securities that results in measuring equity investments at fair value. The adjustment for market risk for loans is intended to capture the risk of unexpected losses,

but not intended to represent fair value, i.e. the proceeds that would be expected to be received if the loans were sold to a market participant. The OFS uses market observable inputs, when available, in developing cash flows and incorporating the adjustment required for market risk. For purposes of this disclosure, the OFS has classified its programs' asset valuations as follows, based on the observability of inputs that are significant to the measurement of the asset:

- Quoted prices for Identical Assets (Level 1): The measurement of assets in this classification is based on direct market quotes for the specific asset, e.g. quoted prices of common stock.

- Significant Observable Inputs (Level 2): The measurement of assets in this classification is primarily derived from market observable data, other than a direct market quote, for the asset. This data could be market quotes for similar assets for the same entity.

- Significant Unobservable Inputs (Level 3): The measurement of assets in this classification is primarily derived from inputs which generally represent management's best estimate of how a market participant would assess the risk inherent in the asset. These unobservable inputs are used because there is little to no direct market activity.

---

[5] The Department of the Treasury retained no ownership interest in AIG at September 30, 2013. It owned 80 million shares of AIG common stock, approximately 5.4 percent of AIG's common stock equity, at September 30, 2012.

The following table displays the assets held by the observability of inputs significant to the measurement of each value:

(Dollars in Millions)	As of September 30, 2013			
	Quoted Prices for Identical Assets (Level 1)	Significant Observable Inputs (Level 2)	Significant Unobservable Inputs (Level 3)	Total
Program				
Capital Purchase Program	$ 125	$ -	$ 1,668	$ 1,793
CDCI and TALF	18	-	451	469
Public-Private Investment Program	-	-	10	10
Automotive Industry Financing Program	3,647	11,950	-	15,597
Total TARP Programs	$ 3,790	$ 11,950	$ 2,129	$ 17,869

(Dollars in Millions)	As of September 30, 2012			
	Quoted Prices for Identical Assets (Level 1)	Significant Observable Inputs (Level 2)	Significant Unobservable Inputs (Level 3)	Total
Program				
Capital Purchase Program	$ 327	$ -	$ 5,407	$ 5,734
CDCI and TALF	9	-	1,095	1,104
Public-Private Investment Program	-	-	10,778	10,778
Automotive Industry Financing Program	11,376	-	6,170	17,546
American International Group Inc. Investment Program	5,067	-	2	5,069
Asset Guarantee Program	-	967	-	967
Total TARP Programs	$ 16,779	$ 967	$ 23,452	$ 41,198

The following provides a description of the methodology used to develop the cash flows and incorporate the market risk into the measurement of the OFS assets.

Financial Institution Equity Investments[6]

The estimated values of preferred equity investments are the net present values of the expected dividend payments and proceeds from repurchases and sales. The model assumes that the key decisions affecting whether or not institutions pay their preferred dividends are made by each institution based on the strength of its balance sheet. The model assumes a probabilistic evolution

[6] This consists of equity investments made under CPP and CDCI.

of each institution's asset-to-liability ratio (the asset-to-liability ratio is based on the estimated fair value of the institution's assets against its liabilities). Each institution's assets are subject to uncertain returns and institutions are assumed to manage their asset-to-liability ratios in such a way that they revert over time to a target level. Historical volatility is used to scale the likely evolution of each institution's asset-to-liability ratio.

In the model, when equity decreases, i.e. the asset-to-liability ratio falls, institutions are increasingly likely to default, either because they enter bankruptcy or are closed by regulators. The probability of default is estimated based on the performance of a large sample of U.S. banks over the period 1990-2012. At the other end of the spectrum, institutions call their preferred shares when the present value of expected future dividends exceeds the call price; this occurs when equity is high and interest rates are low. Inputs to the model include institution-specific accounting data obtained from regulatory filings, an institution's stock price volatility and historical bank failure information, as well as market prices of comparable securities trading in the market. The market risk adjustment is obtained through a calibration process to the market value of certain trading securities of financial institutions within TARP programs or other comparable financial institutions. The OFS estimates the values and projects the cash flows of warrants using an option-pricing approach based on the current stock price and its volatility. Investments in common stock that are exchange traded are valued at the quoted market price as of year end.

Public-Private Investment Program

At September 30, 2013, since the PPIFs no longer held security portfolios, the valuation represents expected proceeds to OFS upon final liquidation of the remaining PPIFs. For the valuations at September 30, 2012, OFS estimated cash flows by simulating the performance of the collateral supporting the residential mortgage-backed securities (RMBS) and commercial mortgage-backed securities (CMBS) held by the PPIF (i.e. performance of the residential and commercial mortgages). Inputs used to simulate the cash flows, which considered market risks, included unemployment forecasts, home price appreciation/depreciation forecasts and the current term structure of interest rates and historical pool performance as well as estimates of the net income and value of commercial real estate supporting the CMBS. The simulated cash flows were then run through a financial model that defined distributions of the RMBS/CMBS to determine the estimated cash flows to the PPIF. Once determined, those cash flows were run through the defined payment hierarchy of the PPIFs to determine the expected cash flows to the OFS through both the equity investments and the loans.

Term Asset-Backed Securities Loan Facility

For TALF, the OFS model derives the cash flows to the Federal Reserve Bank of New York (FRBNY) TALF LLC SPV, and ultimately the OFS, by simulating the performance of underlying collateral. Loss probabilities on the underlying collateral are calculated based on analysis of historical loan loss and charge-off experience by credit sector and subsector. Historical mean loss rates and volatilities are significantly stressed to reflect recent and projected performance. Simulated losses are run through cash flow models to project impairment to the TALF-eligible securities. Simulation outcomes consisting of a range of loss scenarios are probability-weighted to generate the expected net present value of future cash flows.

Automotive Industry Financing Program

Shares of common stock in General Motors Company (New GM) held by OFS were valued by multiplying the publicly traded share price by the number of shares held plus the value of any traded but not settled shares as of September 30, 2013 and 2012. Traded but not settled shares were valued based on the actual trade proceeds.

To value its holdings in Ally at September 30, 2013, OFS considered observable market data from the August 2013 agreement for the repurchase of the Series F-2 and Ally's private offering of new common stock at a price of $6,000 per share. Proceeds and dividends received in November related to the Series F-2 repurchase were discounted to September 30, 2013 at a risk-free discount rate to reflect the timing and certainty of the expected cash flows. OFS's investment in 981,971 shares of common stock was valued at the price per share in Ally's private offering.

To value its holdings in Ally common equity and Series F-2 mandatorily convertible preferred securities, on an "if-converted" basis at September 30, 2012, the OFS used an average of valuation multiples such as price-to-earnings, price-to-tangible book value, and asset manager valuations to estimate the value of the shares. The multiples were based on those of comparable publicly-traded entities. The adjustment for market risk was incorporated in the data points used to determine the measurement for Ally, since all points relied on market data.

American International Group, Inc. Investment Program

The OFS investment in AIG common stock was valued by multiplying the publicly traded share price by the number of shares held as of September

30, 2012. OFS had no investment in AIG common stock remaining as of September 30, 2013.

Asset Guarantee Program

As of September 30, 2012, the instruments within the AGP, consisting of Citigroup Trust Preferred Securities receivable from the FDIC with an $800 million liquidation preference value plus accrued dividends and interest, were valued in a manner broadly analogous to the previously described methodology used for financial institution equity investments. As of September 30, 2013, no instruments remained.

Subsidy Cost and Reestimates

The recorded subsidy cost of a direct loan, equity investment or other credit program is based upon the calculated net present value of expected future cash flows. The OFS's actions, as well as changes in legislation that change these estimated future cash flows change subsidy cost, and are recorded as modifications. The cost or reduction in cost of a modification is recognized when it occurs.

During fiscal year 2013, modifications occurred in the AGP and TALF programs that resulted in subsidy income of $94 million and $55 million, respectively. During fiscal year 2012, a modification occurred in the CPP, increasing subsidy cost by $973 million.

The purpose of reestimates is to update original program subsidy cost estimates to reflect actual cash flow experience as well as changes in equity investment valuations or forecasts of future cash flows. Forecasts of future cash flows are updated based on actual program performance to date, additional information about the portfolio, additional publicly available relevant historical market data on securities performance, revised expectations for future economic conditions, and enhancements to cash flow projection methods.

For fiscal years 2013 and 2012, financial statement reestimates for all programs were performed using actual financial transaction data through September 30. For fiscal years 2013 and 2012, a mix of market and security specific data publicly available as of August 31 and September 30 each year was used for all programs.

Net downward reestimates for the fiscal years ended September 30, 2013 and 2012, totaled $11.8 billion and $11.9 billion, respectively. Descriptions of the reestimates, by OFS Program, are as follows:

CPP

The $1.1 billion downward reestimate for CPP for the year ended September 30, 2013 was the result of a reduction in the projected number of institutions that would be sold via asset sales, repayments and improved market values of the outstanding investments.

The $2.9 billion downward reestimate for CPP for the year ended September 30, 2012 was the result of improved market values of the outstanding investments and the effect of receiving $8.2 billion in repayments, which reduced the remaining investment by about one-half, in fiscal year 2012.

CDCI

The CDCI program continued to experience improved investment performance with several institutions repaying in full, resulting in a $32 million downward reestimate for the year ended September 30, 2013.

The CDCI program reflected improved investment performance, resulting in a $30 million downward reestimate for the year ended September 30, 2012.

PPIP

The $380 million net downward reestimate for the PPIP for the year ended September 30, 2013, was primarily due to accelerated repayments.

The $240 million upward reestimate for the PPIP for the year ended September 30, 2012, was due primarily to accelerated repayments and changes in projected performance of the PPIP portfolio.

TALF

The investments in the TALF continued to experience improved market conditions and accelerated repayments, resulting in a $33 million downward reestimate for the year ended September 30, 2013. The $55 million downward modification reflects principal and interest repayments occurring in February 2013, with contingent interest paid over time beginning in February 2013. Prior to the modification, principal, interest and contingent interest would have occurred in March 2015.

The investments in the TALF experienced improved market conditions and accelerated repayments, resulting in a $96 million downward reestimate for the year ended September 30, 2012.

SBA 7(a)

The SBA 7(a) Securities Purchase Program was closed in fiscal year 2012, with a $1 million downward closing reestimate.

AIFP

Improvements in the common stock share price for New GM accounted for $4.4 billion of the $10.2 billion in downward reestimates for AIFP as of September 30, 2013. The price improved throughout fiscal year 2013, from $22.75 per share at September 30, 2012 to $35.97 per share at September 30, 2013. The remaining $5.8 billion in downward reestimates for AIFP was due to increases in the valuation of the outstanding investment in Ally, reflecting observable market data from the August 2013 agreement for the repurchase of the Series F-2 and for Ally's private offering.

The $230 million upward reestimate for the year ended September 30, 2012, was due to a decline of $1.6 billion in the value of the Ally investment, partially offset by an increase in the common stock market price of New GM, from $20.18 per share at September 30, 2011 to $22.75 per share at September 30, 2012.

AIG Investment Program

The $32 million net upward reestimate for the year ended September 30, 2013 was due primarily to the sale of the remaining 155 million shares of AIG common stock at a price of $32.50 per share, slightly lower than the September 30, 2012 price of $32.79 per share. The AIG program was closed out in fiscal year 2013.

The $9.2 billion downward reestimate for the year ended September 30, 2012 was due primarily to sales of 806 million shares of common stock at prices higher than the September 30, 2011 price of $21.95 per share and the effect of valuing the remaining 155 million shares at the September 30, 2012 price of $32.79 per share.

Summary Table

The following table recaps gross direct loans or equity investments, subsidy allowance, net direct loans or equity investments, reconciliation of subsidy cost allowance and subsidy cost, by TARP program, as of and for the years ended September 30, 2013 and 2012. OFS authority expired October 3, 2010 and no commitments were made thereafter, so there were no budget execution subsidy rates for fiscal years 2013 and 2012.

Troubled Asset Relief Program Loans and Equity Investments
(Dollars in Millions)

	TOTAL	CPP	PPIP	AIFP	AIG	CDCI-TALF
As of September 30, 2013						
Direct Loans and Equity Investment Programs:						
Direct Loans and Equity Investments Outstanding, Gross	$ 23,496	$ 3,143	$ -	$ 19,878	$ -	$ 475
Subsidy Cost Allowance	(5,627)	(1,350)	10	(4,281)	-	(6)
Direct Loans and Equity Investments Outstanding, Net	$ 17,869	$ 1,793	$ 10	$ 15,597	$ -	$ 469
Obligations for Loans and Investments not yet Disbursed	$ 984	$ -	$ 984	$ -	$ -	$ -
Reconciliation of Subsidy Cost Allowance:						
Balance, Beginning of Period	$ 22,842	$ 2,930	$ (1,015)	$ 19,706	$ 1,658	$ (437)
Subsidy Cost (Income) for Modifications	(55)	-	-	-	-	(55)
Dividend and Interest Income	1,092	262	271	534	-	25
Net Proceeds from Sales and Repurchases of Assets in Excess of (Less than) Cost	(5,790)	(493)	1,173	(5,361)	(1,679)	570
Write-Offs	(111)	(104)	-	-	-	(7)
Net Interest Expense on Borrowings from Fiscal Service and Financing Account Balance	(612)	(105)	(59)	(412)	(11)	(25)
Balance, End of Period, Before Reestimates	17,366	2,490	370	14,467	(32)	71
Subsidy Reestimates - Upward (Downward)	(11,739)	(1,140)	(380)	(10,186)	32	(65)
Balance, End of Period	$ 5,627	$ 1,350	$ (10)	$ 4,281	$ -	$ 6
Reconciliation of Subsidy Cost (Income):						
Subsidy Cost (Income) for Modifications	$ (55)	$ -	$ -	$ -	$ -	$ (55)
Subsidy Reestimates - Upward (Downward)	(11,739)	(1,140)	(380)	(10,186)	32	(65)
Total Direct Loan and Equity Investment Programs Subsidy Cost (Income)	$ (11,794)	$ (1,140)	$ (380)	$ (10,186)	$ 32	$ (120)

(Dollars in Millions)

	TOTAL	CPP	PPIP	AIFP	AIG	CDCI-TALF-SBA
As of September 30, 2012						
Direct Loans and Equity Investment Programs:						
Direct Loans and Equity Investments Outstanding, Gross	$ 63,073	$ 8,664	$ 9,763	$ 37,252	$ 6,727	$ 667
Subsidy Cost Allowance	(22,842)	(2,930)	1,015	(19,706)	(1,658)	437
Direct Loans and Equity Investments Outstanding, Net	$ 40,231	$ 5,734	$ 10,778	$ 17,546	$ 5,069	$ 1,104
New Loans or Investments Disbursed	$ 1,048	$ -	$ 1,048	$ -	$ -	$ -
Obligations for Loans and Investments not yet Disbursed	$ 4,358	$ -	$ 3,058	$ -	$ -	$ 1,300
Reconciliation of Subsidy Cost Allowance:						
Balance, Beginning of Period	$ 42,301	$ 4,857	$ (2,434)	$ 19,440	$ 20,717	$ (279)
Subsidy Cost (Income) for Disbursements and Modifications	942	973	(31)	-	-	-
Dividend and Interest Income	2,733	572	1,426	534	191	10
Net Proceeds from Sales and Repurchases of Assets in Excess of (Less than) Cost	(9,788)	(285)	223	9	(9,735)	-
Net Interest Expense on Borrowings from Fiscal Service and Financing Account Balance	(1,626)	(290)	(439)	(507)	(349)	(41)
Balance, End of Period, Before Reestimates	34,562	5,827	(1,255)	19,476	10,824	(310)
Subsidy Reestimates - Upward (Downward)	(11,720)	(2,897)	240	230	(9,166)	(127)
Balance, End of Period	$ 22,842	$ 2,930	$ (1,015)	$ 19,706	$ 1,658	$ (437)
Reconciliation of Subsidy Cost (Income):						
Subsidy Cost (Income) for Disbursements	$ (31)	$ -	$ (31)	$ -	$ -	$ -
Subsidy Cost (Income) for Modifications	973	973	-	-	-	-
Subsidy Reestimates - Upward (Downward)	(11,720)	(2,897)	240	230	(9,166)	(127)
Total Direct Loan and Equity Investment Programs Subsidy Cost (Income)	$ (10,778)	$ (1,924)	$ 209	$ 230	$ (9,166)	$ (127)

Other Credit Programs

Asset Guarantee Program

The Asset Guarantee Program (AGP) provided guarantees for assets held by systemically significant financial institutions that faced a risk of losing market confidence due in large part to a portfolio of distressed or illiquid assets.

Section 102 of the EESA required the Secretary to establish the AGP to guarantee troubled assets originated or issued prior to March 14, 2008, including mortgage-backed securities. The OFS completed its only transaction under the AGP in January 2009, when it finalized the terms of a guarantee agreement with Citigroup. Under the agreement, the OFS, the Federal Deposit Insurance Corporation (FDIC), and the FRBNY (collectively the USG Parties) provided protection against the possibility of large losses on an asset pool of approximately $301.0 billion of loans and securities backed by residential and commercial real estate and other such assets, which remained on Citigroup's balance sheet. The OFS's guarantee was limited to $5.0 billion.

As a premium for the guarantee, Citigroup issued $7.0 billion of cumulative perpetual preferred stock (subsequently converted to Trust Preferred Securities with similar terms) with an 8 percent stated dividend rate and a warrant for the purchase of common stock; $4.0 billion and the warrant were issued to the OFS, and $3.0 billion was issued to the FDIC.

In December 2009, the USG Parties and Citigroup agreed to terminate the guarantee agreement. Citigroup cancelled $1.8 billion of the preferred stock previously issued to OFS. In addition, the FDIC agreed to transfer to the OFS $800 million of their Trust Preferred Securities (TruPS) plus dividends by December 31, 2012. The amount OFS was to receive would be reduced by any losses FDIC incurred on its Citigroup guaranteed debt. The additional preferred shares from the FDIC were included in the subsidy calculation for AGP, based on the net present value of expected future cash inflows.

Only the $800 million of TruPS-related receivable from the FDIC valued at $967 million was on the OFS Balance Sheet at September 30, 2012. The TruPS were received, exchanged for subordinated notes, and the notes sold in 2013 for $894 million. In addition, OFS received $200 million of dividends on the TruPS in 2013 and the program was closed.

A downward modification of $94 million due to the exchange of TruPS into subordinated notes and immediate sale of the notes, and net reestimates including the closing downward reestimate of $24 million resulted in subsidy income for fiscal year 2013. For fiscal year 2012, the AGP program recorded a $207 million downward reestimate, due to revised expectations about the timing of receipt of dividends, interest on the dividends and the TruPS from the FDIC.

The following table details the changes in the receivable account and the AGP subsidy cost during fiscal years 2013 and 2012:

Reconciliation of Asset Guarantee Program Receivable:

		Fiscal Year		
(Dollars in Millions)		2013		2012
Balance, Beginning of Period	$	967	$	739
Subsidy Income for Modifications		94		-
Dividend Revenue		(200)		-
Proceeds from Sales in Excess of Cost		(894)		-
Net Interest Expense on Borrowings from Fiscal Service and Financing Account Balance		9		21
Balance, End of Period, Before Reestimates		(24)		760
Subsidy Reestimates - Downward		24		207
Balance, End of Period	$	-	$	967

Reconciliation of Subsidy Cost (Income):

Subsidy Income for Modifications	$	(94)		-
Subsidy Reestimates - (Downward)		(24)		(207)
Total Subsidy Cost (Income)	$	(118)	$	(207)

FHA-Refinance Program

The OFS entered into a loss-sharing agreement with the FHA to support a program in which FHA guarantees refinancing of borrowers whose homes were worth less than the remaining amounts owed under their mortgage loans. OFS has established a $50 million account, held by a commercial bank serving as its agent, from which any required reimbursements for losses will be paid to third party claimants, including banks or other investors.

During fiscal year 2013, $182 million of loans were disbursed by the FHA. As of September 30, 2013, 3,015 loans that FHA guaranteed, with a total value of $489 million, had been refinanced under the program through May 2013. Effective June 1, 2013, the Treasury Coverage Ratio, which governs the amount of losses financed by OFS, was recalculated and it was determined that OFS's guarantee was no longer needed during the remainder of fiscal year 2013. During fiscal year 2012, $234 million of loans were disbursed by the FHA. As of September 30, 2012, 1,774 loans that FHA had guaranteed, with a total value of $307 million, had been refinanced under the program.

OFS's maximum exposure related to FHA's guarantee totaled $59 million and $41 million at September 30, 2013 and 2012, respectively. OFS's guarantee resulted in a liability of $9 million at September 30, 2013 and a liability of $7 million at September 30, 2012. The liability was calculated, using credit reform accounting, as the present value of the estimated future cash outflows for the OFS's share of losses incurred on any defaults of the disbursed loans. As of September 30, 2013, $47,840 of claims had been paid by OFS under the program. As of September 30, 2012, no claims had been paid.

At September 30, 2013, OFS's obligation for subsidy for undisbursed loans was $1.0 billion. This was reduced in fiscal year 2013 from the $8.1 billion outstanding at September 30, 2012, due to adjustments to expected participation in the program.

Budget subsidy rates for the program, entirely for defaults, were set at 2.48 percent and 4.0 percent for loans guaranteed in fiscal years 2013 and 2012, respectively.

The program recorded $3 million downward reestimates each year, for fiscal years 2013 and 2012, due to reductions in market risks and lower than projected defaults.

The following table details the changes in the FHA-Refinance Program Liability and the Subsidy Cost for the program during fiscal years 2013 and 2012:

Reconciliation of FHA- Refinance Program Liability

	Fiscal Year	
(Dollars in Millions)	2013	2012
Balance, Beginning of Period	$ 7	$ 1
Subsidy Cost for Guarantees (Defaults)	5	9
Balance, End of Period, Before Reestimates	12	10
Subsidy Reestimates - (Downward)	(3)	(3)
Balance, End of Period	$ 9	$ 7

Reconciliation of Subsidy Cost (Income)

Subsidy Cost for Guarantees (Defaults)	$ 5	$ 9
Subsidy Reestimates - (Downward)	(3)	(3)
Total Subsidy Cost (Income)	$ 2	$ 6

NOTE 7. DUE TO THE GENERAL FUND

As of September 30, 2013, the OFS accrued $8.1 billion of downward reestimates payable to the General Fund. As of September 30, 2012, the OFS accrued $9.7 billion of downward reestimates payable to the General Fund. Due to the General Fund is a Non-Entity liability on the Balance Sheet.

NOTE 8. PRINCIPAL PAYABLE TO THE BUREAU OF THE FISCAL SERVICE (Fiscal Service)

Equity investments, direct loans and other credit programs accounted for under federal credit reform are funded by subsidy appropriations and borrowings from the Fiscal Service. The OFS also borrows funds to pay the Treasury General Fund for negative program subsidy costs and downward reestimates (these reduce program subsidy cost) in advance of receiving the expected cash flows that cause the negative program subsidy or downward reestimate. The OFS makes periodic principal repayments to the Fiscal Service based on the analysis of its cash balances and future disbursement needs. All debt is intragovernmental and covered by budgetary resources. See additional details on borrowing authority in Note 11, Statement of Budgetary Resources.

Debt transactions for the fiscal years ended September 30, 2013 and 2012, were as follows:

| (Dollars in Millions) | As of September 30, | |
	2013	2012
Beginning Balance, Principal Payable to the Fiscal Service	$ 52,828	$ 129,497
New Borrowings	208	2,658
Repayments	(41,087)	(79,327)
Ending Balance, Principal Payable to the Fiscal Service	$ 11,949	$ 52,828

Borrowings from the Fiscal Service by TARP program, outstanding as of September 30, 2013 and 2012, were as follows:

| (Dollars in Millions) | As of September 30, | |
	2013	2012
Capital Purchase Program	$ 1,210	$ 5,150
CDCI and TALF	551	1,020
Public-Private Investment Program	305	16,317
Automotive Industry Financing Program	9,883	17,845
American International Group, Inc. Investment Program	-	11,736
Asset Guarantee Program	-	760
Total Borrowings Outstanding	$ 11,949	$ 52,828

As of September 30, 2013, borrowings carried remaining terms ranging from 3 to 28 years, with interest rates from 2.5 percent to 3.8 percent. As of September 30, 2012, borrowings carried remaining terms ranging from 2 to 29 years, with interest rates from 1.0 percent to 4.4 percent.

NOTE 9. COMMITMENTS AND CONTINGENCIES

The OFS is party to various legal actions and claims brought by or against it. In the opinion of management and the Chief Counsel, the ultimate resolution of these legal actions and claims will not have a material effect on the OFS financial statements. The OFS has not incurred any loss contingencies that would be considered probable or reasonably possible for these cases; therefore, no liability was established. Refer to Note 5 for additional commitments relating to the Treasury Housing Programs under TARP and Note 6 relating to Direct Loans and Equity Investments, Net and Other Credit Programs.

NOTE 10. STATEMENT OF NET COST

The Statement of Net Cost (SNC) presents the net cost of (income from) operations for the OFS under the strategic goal of ensuring the overall stability and liquidity of the financial system, preventing avoidable foreclosures and preserving homeownership. The OFS has determined that all initiatives and programs under the TARP fall within this strategic goal.

The OFS SNC reports the annual accumulated full cost of the TARP's output, including both direct and indirect costs of the program services and output identifiable to TARP, in accordance with SFFAS No. 4, *Managerial Cost Accounting Concepts and Standards.*

The OFS SNC for fiscal year 2013 includes $856 million of intragovernmental costs relating to interest expense on borrowings from the Fiscal Service and $235 million intragovernmental revenues relating to interest income on financing account balances. The OFS SNC for fiscal year 2012 includes $2.3 billion of intragovernmental costs relating to interest expense on borrowings from the Fiscal Service and $605 million in intragovernmental revenues relating to interest income on financing account balances.

Subsidy allowance amortization on the SNC is the difference between interest income on financing fund account balances, dividends and interest income on direct loans, equity investments and other credit programs from TARP participants, and interest expense on borrowings from the Fiscal Service. Credit reform accounting requires that only subsidy cost, not the net of other costs (interest expense and dividend and interest income), be reflected in the SNC. The subsidy allowance account is used to present the loan or equity investment at the estimated net present value of future cash flows. The OFS SNC includes $671 million and $1.1 billion of subsidy allowance amortization for fiscal years 2013 and 2012, respectively.

NOTE 11. STATEMENT OF BUDGETARY RESOURCES

The Statement of Budgetary Resources (SBR) presents information about total budgetary resources available to the OFS and the status of those resources. For the year ended September 30, 2013, the OFS's total resources in budgetary accounts were $22.4 billion and resources in non-budgetary financing accounts, including borrowing authority and spending authority from collections of loan principal, liquidation of equity investments, interest, dividends and fees were $15.6 billion. For the year ended September 30, 2012, the OFS's total resources in budgetary accounts were $41.9 billion and resources in non-budgetary financing accounts were $25.9 billion.

Permanent Indefinite Appropriations

The OFS receives permanent indefinite appropriations annually, if necessary, to fund increases in the projected subsidy costs of direct loans, equity investments and other credit programs as determined by the reestimation process required by the FCRA.

Additionally, Section 118 of the EESA states that the Secretary may issue public debt securities and use the resulting funds to carry out the Act and that any such funds expended or obligated by the

Secretary for actions authorized by this Act, including the payment of administrative expenses, shall be deemed appropriated at the time of such expenditure or obligation.

Borrowing Authority

The OFS is authorized to borrow from the Fiscal Service whenever funds needed to disburse direct loans and equity investments, and to enter into asset guarantee and loss-sharing arrangements, exceed subsidy costs and collections in the non-budgetary financing accounts. For the year ended September 30, 2013, the OFS had no borrowing authority available, of the $208 million authorized, since the authority was used. For the year ended September 30, 2012, the OFS had borrowing authority available of $2.6 billion, of the $2.7 billion authorized.

The OFS uses dividends and interest received as well as principal repayments on direct loans and liquidation of equity investments to repay debt in the non-budgetary direct loan, equity investment and other credit program financing accounts. These receipts are not available for any other use per credit reform accounting guidance.

Apportionment Categories of Obligations Incurred: Direct versus Reimbursable Obligations

All of the OFS apportionments are Direct and are Category B. Category B apportionments typically distribute budgetary resources on a basis other than calendar quarters, such as by activities, projects, objects or a combination of these categories. The OFS obligations incurred are direct obligations (obligations not financed from intragovernmental reimbursable agreements).

Undelivered Orders

Undelivered orders as of September 30, 2013 were $29.1 billion in budgetary accounts and $1.0 billion in non-budgetary financing accounts. Undelivered orders as of September 30, 2012 were $40.2 billion in budgetary accounts and $5.9 billion in non-budgetary financing accounts.

Explanation of Differences Between the Statement of Budgetary Resources and the Budget of the United States Government

Federal agencies and entities are required to explain material differences between amounts reported in the SBR and the actual amounts reported in the Budget of the U.S. Government (the President's Budget).

The President's Budget for 2015, with the "Actual" column completed for fiscal year 2013, has not yet been published as of the date of these financial statements. The President's Budget is currently expected to be published and delivered to Congress in early February 2014. It will be available from the Government Printing Office.

The 2014 President's Budget, with the "Actual" column completed for the year ended September 30, 2012, was published in April 2013, and reconciled to the SBR. The only differences between the two documents were due to:
- Rounding;
- Expired funds that are not shown in the "Actual" column of the President's Budget.

NOTE 12. RECONCILIATION OF OBLIGATIONS INCURRED TO NET COST OF (INCOME FROM) OPERATIONS

The OFS presents the SNC using the accrual basis of accounting. This differs from the obligation-based measurement of total resources supplied, both budgetary and from other sources, on the SBR. The reconciliation of obligations incurred to net cost of operations shown below categorizes the differences between the two, and illustrates that the OFS maintains reconcilable consistency between the two types of reporting.

The Reconciliation of Obligations Incurred to Net Cost of (Income from) Operations for the fiscal years ended September 30, 2013 and 2012 follows:

(Dollars in Millions)	2013	2012
Resources Used to Finance Activities:		
Budgetary Resources Obligated		
Obligations Incurred	$ 14,879	$ 35,803
Actual Offsetting Collections, Net of Change in Uncollected Customer Payments, and Recoveries	(48,668)	(87,383)
Offsetting Receipts	(13,218)	(6,063)
Net Obligations	(47,007)	(57,643)
Other Resources	1	1
Total Resources Used to Finance Activities	(47,006)	(57,642)
Resources Used to Finance Items Not Part of Net Cost of (Income from) Operations:		
Net Obligations in Direct Loan, Equity Investment and Other Credit Programs Financing Funds	27,322	78,988
Change in Resources Obligated for Goods, Services and Benefits Ordered but not yet Provided	11,164	3,157
Resources that Fund Prior Period Expenses and Reestimates	8,957	(23,294)
Total Resources Used to Finance Items Not Part of Net Cost of (Income from) Operations	47,443	58,851
Total Resources Used to Finance the Net Cost of (Income from) Operations	437	1,209
Components of Net Cost of (Income from) Operations that Will Not Require or Generate Resources in the Current Period:		
Accrued Net Downward Reestimates at Year-End	(8,139)	(8,958)
Other	1	1
Total Components of Net Cost of (Income from) Operations that Will Not Require or Generate Resources in the Current Period	(8,138)	(8,957)
Net Cost of (Income from) Operations	$ (7,701)	$ (7,748)

Office of Financial Stability - Troubled Asset Relief Program

REQUIRED SUPPLEMENTARY INFORMATION
COMBINED STATEMENT OF BUDGETARY RESOURCES
For the Year Ended September 30, 2013

(Unaudited)

| | 2013 | | | | | |
| | Combined | | TARP Programs | | TARP Administrative | |
Dollars in Millions	Budgetary Accounts	Nonbudgetary Financing Accounts	Budgetary Accounts	Nonbudgetary Financing Accounts	Budgetary Accounts	Nonbudgetary Financing Accounts
BUDGETARY RESOURCES						
Unobligated Balances Brought Forward, October 1	$ 14,350	$ 17,631	$ 14,071	$ 17,631	$ 279	$ -
Recoveries of Prior-Year Unpaid Obligations	7,246	4,941	7,219	4,941	27	
Borrowing Authority Withdrawn	-	(2,611)	-	(2,611)		
Actual Repayment of Debt, Prior-Year Balances	-	(17,738)	-	(17,738)	-	
Unobligated Balance from Prior-Year Budget Authority, Net	21,596	2,223	21,290	2,223	306	
Appropriations	788	-	483	-	305	-
Borrowing Authority	-	208	-	208	-	-
Spending Authority from Offsetting Collections	1	13,131	-	13,131	1	
TOTAL BUDGETARY RESOURCES (Note 11)	**$ 22,385**	**$ 15,562**	**$ 21,773**	**$ 15,562**	**$ 612**	**$ -**
STATUS OF BUDGETARY RESOURCES						
Obligations Incurred	$ 779	$ 14,100	$ 483	$ 14,100	$ 296	$ -
Unobligated Balance:						
Apportioned	11	668	-	668	11	
Unapportioned	21,595	794	21,290	794	305	
Total Unobligated Balance	21,606	1,462	21,290	1,462	316	
TOTAL STATUS OF BUDGETARY RESOURCES	**$ 22,385**	**$ 15,562**	**$ 21,773**	**$ 15,562**	**$ 612**	**$ -**
CHANGE IN OBLIGATED BALANCES						
Unpaid Obligations:						
Unpaid Obligations Brought Forward, October 1	$ 40,548	$ 5,926	$ 40,384	$ 5,926	$ 164	$ -
Obligations Incurred	779	14,100	483	14,100	296	
Gross Outlays	(4,675)	(14,092)	(4,427)	(14,092)	(248)	
Recoveries of Prior-Year Unpaid Obligations	(7,246)	(4,941)	(7,219)	(4,941)	(27)	
Unpaid Obligations, End of Year	29,406	993	29,221	993	185	-
Uncollected Payments from Federal Sources:						
Uncollected Payments Brought Forward, October 1	-	(349)	-	(349)	-	-
Change in Uncollected Payments	-	123	-	123	-	-
Uncollected Payments from Federal Sources, End of Year	-	(226)	-	(226)	-	-
Obligated Balance, Net, End of Year	**$ 29,406**	**$ 767**	**$ 29,221**	**$ 767**	**$ 185**	**$ -**
OBLIGATED BALANCES						
(Net of Unpaid Obligations and Uncollected Payments Above)						
Obligated Balance, Net, Brought Forward, October 1	**$ 40,548**	**$ 5,577**	**$ 40,384**	**$ 5,577**	**$ 164**	**$ -**
Obligated Balance, Net, End of Year	**$ 29,406**	**$ 767**	**$ 29,221**	**$ 767**	**$ 185**	**$ -**
BUDGET AUTHORITY AND OUTLAYS, NET						
Budget Authority, Gross	$ 789	$ 13,339	$ 483	$ 13,339	$ 306	$ -
Actual Offsetting Collections	(1)	(36,604)	-	(36,604)	(1)	
Change in Uncollected Customer Payments from Federal Sources	-	123	-	123	-	
BUDGET AUTHORITY, NET	**$ 788**	**$ (23,142)**	**$ 483**	**$ (23,142)**	**$ 305**	**$ -**
Gross Outlays	$ 4,675	$ 14,092	$ 4,427	$ 14,092	$ 248	$ -
Actual Offsetting Collections	(1)	(36,604)	-	(36,604)	(1)	
Net Outlays	4,674	(22,512)	4,427	(22,512)	247	
Distributed Offsetting Receipts	(13,218)	-	(13,218)	-	-	
AGENCY OUTLAYS, NET	**$ (8,544)**	**$ (22,512)**	**$ (8,791)**	**$ (22,512)**	**$ 247**	**$ -**

Office of Financial Stability - Troubled Asset Relief Program
REQUIRED SUPPLEMENTARY INFORMATION
COMBINED STATEMENT OF BUDGETARY RESOURCES
For the Year Ended September 30, 2012
(Unaudited)

	2012					
	Combined		TARP Programs		TARP Administrative	
Dollars in Millions	Budgetary Accounts	Nonbudgetary Financing Accounts	Budgetary Accounts	Nonbudgetary Financing Accounts	Budgetary Accounts	Nonbudgetary Financing Accounts
BUDGETARY RESOURCES						
Unobligated Balance Brought Forward, October 1	$ 14,166 $	21,143 $	13,967 $	21,143 $	199 $	-
Recoveries of Prior-Year Unpaid Obligations	146	6,114	104	6,114	42	-
Borrowing Authority Withdrawn	-	(5,832)	-	(5,832)		
Actual Repayment of Debt, Prior-Year Balances	-	(19,900)	-	(19,900)		
Unobligated Balance from Prior-Year Budget Authority, Net	14,312	1,525	14,071	1,525	241	-
Appropriations	27,593	-	27,270	-	323	-
Borrowing Authority	-	2,659	-	2,659	-	-
Spending Authority from Offsetting Collections	-	21,695	-	21,695	-	
TOTAL BUDGETARY RESOURCES (Note 11)	**$ 41,905 $**	**25,879 $**	**41,341 $**	**25,879 $**	**564 $**	**-**
STATUS OF BUDGETARY RESOURCES						
Obligations Incurred	$ 27,555 $	8,248 $	27,270 $	8,248 $	285 $	-
Unobligated Balance:						
Apportioned	41	3,946	-	3,946	41	
Unapportioned	14,309	13,685	14,071	13,685	238	-
Total Unobligated Balance	14,350	17,631	14,071	17,631	279	-
TOTAL STATUS OF BUDGETARY RESOURCES	**$ 41,905 $**	**25,879 $**	**41,341 $**	**25,879 $**	**564 $**	**-**
CHANGE IN OBLIGATED BALANCES						
Unpaid Obligations:						
Unpaid Obligations Brought Forward, October 1	$ 43,814 $	13,158 $	43,618 $	13,158 $	196 $	-
Obligations Incurred	27,555	8,248	27,270	8,248	285	
Gross Outlays	(30,675)	(9,366)	(30,400)	(9,366)	(275)	
Recoveries of Prior-Year Unpaid Obligations	(146)	(6,114)	(104)	(6,114)	(42)	
Unpaid Obligations, End of Year	40,548	5,926	40,384	5,926	164	-
Uncollected Payments from Federal Sources:						
Uncollected Payments Brought Forward, October 1	-	(496)	-	(496)	-	-
Change in Uncollected Payments	-	147	-	147	-	-
Uncollected Payments from Federal Sources, End of Year	-	(349)	-	(349)	-	-
Obligated Balance, Net, End of Year	**$ 40,548 $**	**5,577 $**	**40,384 $**	**5,577 $**	**164 $**	**-**
OBLIGATED BALANCES						
(Net of Unpaid Obligations and Uncollected Payments Above)						
Obligated Balance, Net, Brought Forward, October 1	**$ 43,814 $**	**12,662 $**	**43,618 $**	**12,662 $**	**196 $**	**-**
Obligated Balance, Net, End of Year	**$ 40,548 $**	**5,577 $**	**40,384 $**	**5,577 $**	**164 $**	**-**
BUDGET AUTHORITY AND OUTLAYS, NET						
Budget Authority, Gross	$ 27,593 $	24,354 $	27,270 $	24,354 $	323 $	-
Actual Offsetting Collections	-	(81,269)	-	(81,269)	-	-
Change in Uncollected Customer Payments from Federal Sources	-	147	-	147	-	-
BUDGET AUTHORITY, NET	**$ 27,593 $**	**(56,768) $**	**27,270 $**	**(56,768) $**	**323 $**	**-**
Gross Outlays	$ 30,675 $	9,366 $	30,400 $	9,366 $	275 $	-
Actual Offsetting Collections	-	(81,269)	-	(81,269)	-	-
Net Outlays	30,675	(71,903)	30,400	(71,903)	275	-
Distributed Offsetting Receipts	(6,063)	-	(6,063)	-	-	-
AGENCY OUTLAYS, NET	**$ 24,612 $**	**(71,903) $**	**24,337 $**	**(71,903) $**	**275 $**	**-**

Office of Financial Stability - Troubled Asset Relief Program

OTHER INFORMATION
SCHEDULE OF SPENDING
For the Years Ended September 30, 2013 and 2012
(Unaudited)

Dollars in Millions	2013 Budgetary Accounts	2013 Nonbudgetary Financing Accounts	2012 Budgetary Accounts	2012 Nonbudgetary Financing Accounts
WHAT IS AVAILABLE TO SPEND?				
Total Resources per Statement of Budgetary Resources (SBR)	$ 22,385	$ 15,562	$ 41,905	$ 25,879
Less Amount Apportioned (not yet agreed to be spent)	(11)	(668)	(41)	(3,946)
Less Amount Unapportioned (not yet available to be spent)	(21,595)	(794)	(14,309)	(13,685)
AMOUNT AVAILABLE TO SPEND- OBLIGATIONS INCURRED PER SBR	$ 779	$ 14,100	$ 27,555	$ 8,248
HOW WAS THE AMOUNT SPENT?				
Personnel Compensation	$ 17	$ -	$ 22	$ -
Personnel Benefits	5	-	6	-
Travel and Transportation	1	-	1	-
Supplies and Materials	1	-	2	-
Other Services	272	26	254	20
Interest	-	856	-	2,252
Subsidies, including Reestimates for Previously Disbursed Loans and Investments Outstanding[7]	483	13,218	27,270	5,976
AMOUNT AVAILABLE TO SPEND- OBLIGATIONS INCURRED PER SBR	$ 779	$ 14,100	$ 27,555	$ 8,248
TO WHOM WERE THE OBLIGATIONS MADE?				
Federal Agencies and Entities	$ 505	$ 14,074	$ 27,306	$ 8,228
Non-Federal Companies - Freddie Mac/Fannie Mae for Housing	215	-	164	-
Non-Federal Companies - All Other	41	26	60	20
Non-Federal Individuals	18	-	25	-
AMOUNT AVAILABLE TO SPEND- OBLIGATIONS INCURRED PER SBR	$ 779	$ 14,100	$ 27,555	$ 8,248

The Schedule of Spending presents an overview of obligations incurred subtotaled by purpose and again by type of entity to be paid. Obligations are legally binding agreements that usually result in outlays, immediately or in the future. The schedule presents more detail than the Statement of Budgetary Resources, although the data used to populate both is the same.

The section "How Was the Amount Spent" presents obligations committed to in each fiscal year for services received, supplies purchased, subsidies and program loans or investments made, even if actual receipt of services or goods has not yet occurred or

payments have not yet been made for particular obligations. While most obligations become contractual agreements for which services and goods are received in the same fiscal year as established, certain obligations or portions of obligations reported here may never be used. These unused amounts, when closed, are reported as "Recoveries of Prior-Year Unpaid Obligations" on the SBR.

---

[7] Subsidies obligated in nonbudgetary financing accounts consist of negative subsidies and downward reestimates, which are reductions of subsidy cost, transferred from the financing accounts to the Treasury General Fund. These transfers occur in the same fiscal year as the obligations.

APPENDIX A: TARP GLOSSARY

Asset-Backed Security (ABS): A financial instrument representing an interest in a pool of other assets, typically consumer loans. Most ABS are backed by credit card receivables, auto loans, student loans, or other loan and lease obligations.

Asset Guarantee Program (AGP): A TARP program under which OFS, together with the Federal Reserve and the FDIC, agreed to share losses on certain pools of assets held by systemically significant financial institutions that faced a high risk of losing market confidence due in large part to a portfolio of distressed or illiquid assets.

Automotive Industry Financing Program (AIFP): A TARP program under which OFS provided loans or equity investments in order to avoid a disorderly bankruptcy of one or more auto companies that would have posed a systemic risk to the country's financial system.

Capital Purchase Program (CPP): A TARP program pursuant to which OFS invested in preferred equity securities and other securities issued by financial institutions.

Commercial Mortgage-Backed Securities (CMBS): A financial instrument representing an interest in a commercial real estate mortgage or a group of commercial real estate mortgages.

Community Development Capital Initiative (CDCI): A TARP program that provides low-cost capital to Community Development Financial Institutions to encourage lending to small businesses and help facilitate the flow of credit to individuals in underserved communities.

Community Development Financial Institution (CDFI): A financial institution that focuses on providing financial services to low- and moderate- income, minority and other underserved communities, and is certified by the CDFI Fund, an office within

OFS that promotes economic revitalization and community development.

Debtor-In-Possession (DIP): A debtor-in-possession in U. S. bankruptcy law has filed a bankruptcy petition but still remains in possession of its property. DIP financing usually has priority over existing debt, equity and other claims.

Emergency Economic Stabilization Act (EESA): The law that created the Troubled Asset Relief Program (TARP).

Government-Sponsored Enterprises (GSEs): Private corporations created by the U.S. Government. Fannie Mae and Freddie Mac are GSEs.

Home Affordable Modification Program (HAMP): A TARP program OFS established to help responsible but struggling homeowners reduce their mortgage payments to affordable levels and avoid foreclosure.

Legacy Securities: CMBS and non-agency RMBS issued prior to 2009 that were originally rated AAA or an equivalent rating by two or more nationally recognized statistical rating organizations without ratings enhancement and that are secured directly by actual mortgage loans, leases or other assets and not other securities.

Making Home Affordable (MHA): A comprehensive plan to stabilize the U.S. housing market and help responsible, but struggling, homeowners reduce their monthly mortgage payments to more affordable levels and avoid foreclosure. HAMP is part of MHA.

Mortgage-Backed Securities (MBS): A type of ABS representing an interest in a pool of similar mortgages bundled together by a financial institution.

Non-Agency Residential Mortgage-Backed Securities: RMBS that are not guaranteed or issued by Freddie Mac, Fannie Mae, any other

GSE, Ginnie Mae, or a U.S. federal government agency.

Preferred Stock: Equity ownership that usually pays a fixed dividend and gives the holder a claim on corporate earnings superior to common stock owners. Preferred stock also has priority in the distribution of assets in the case of liquidation of a bankrupt company.

Public-Private Investment Fund (PPIF): An investment fund established to purchase Legacy Securities from financial institutions under PPIP.

Public-Private Investment Program (PPIP): A TARP program designed to support the secondary market in mortgage-backed securities. The program is designed to increase the flow of credit throughout the economy by partnering with private investors to purchase Legacy Securities from financial institutions.

Qualifying Financial Institution (QFI): Private and public U.S.-controlled banks, savings associations, bank holding companies, certain savings and loan holding companies, and mutual organizations.

Residential Mortgage-Backed Securities (RMBS): A financial instrument representing an interest in a group of residential real estate mortgages.

SBA: U.S. Small Business Administration.

SBA 7(a) Securities Purchase Program: A TARP program under which OFS purchased securities backed by the guaranteed portions of the SBA 7(a) loans.

Servicer: An administrative third party that collects mortgage payments, handles tax and insurance escrows, and may even bring foreclosure proceedings on past due mortgages for institutional loan owners or originators. The loan servicer also generates reports for borrowers and mortgage owners on the collections.

Targeted Investment Program (TIP): A TARP program created to stabilize the financial system by making investments in institutions that are critical to the functioning of the financial system.

Term Asset-Backed Securities Loan Facility (TALF): A program under which the Federal Reserve Bank of New York made term non-recourse loans to buyers of AAA-rated Asset-Backed Securities in order to stimulate consumer and business lending.

Troubled Asset Relief Program (TARP): The Troubled Asset Relief Program, which was established under EESA to help stabilize the financial system and prevent a systemic collapse.

Trust Preferred Security (TruPS): A security that has both equity and debt characteristics, created by establishing a trust and issuing debt to it. TruPS are treated as capital, not debt, for regulatory purposes.

Warrant: A financial instrument that represents the right, but not the obligation, to purchase a certain number of shares of common stock of a company at a fixed price.

APPENDIX B: ABBREVIATIONS AND ACRONYMS

ABS	Asset-Backed Securities		**QFI**	Qualifying Financial Institution
AGP	Asset Guarantee Program		**RMBS**	Residential Mortgage-Backed Securities
AIFP	Automotive Industry Financing Program		**SCAP**	Supervisory Capital Assessment Program
AIG	American International Group, Inc.		**SIGTARP**	Special Inspector General for the Troubled Asset Relief Program
CAP	Capital Assistance Program		**SPV**	Special Purpose Vehicle
CDFI	Community Development Financial Institution		**TAIFF**	Troubled Assets Insurance Financing Fund
CMBS	Commercial Mortgage-Backed Securities		**TALF**	Term Asset-Backed Securities Loan Facility
CP	Commercial Paper		**TARP**	Troubled Asset Relief Program
COP	Congressional Oversight Panel		**TIP**	Targeted Investment Program
CPP	Capital Purchase Program		**TruPS**	Trust Preferred Securities
CDCI	Community Development Capital Initiative		**USDA**	U. S. Department of Agriculture
DIP	Debtor-In-Possession			
EESA	Emergency Economic Stabilization Act of 2008			
FCRA	Federal Credit Reform Act of 1990			
FHA	Federal Housing Administration			
FRBNY	Federal Reserve Bank of New York			
GAO	Government Accountability Office			
GSE	Government-Sponsored Enterprise			
HAFA	Home Affordable Foreclosure Alternatives			
HHF	Hardest Hit Fund			
HAMP	Home Affordable Modification Program			
HPDP	Home Price Decline Protection			
MBS	Mortgage-Backed Security			
MHA	Making Home Affordable Program			
OFS	Office of Financial Stability			
OMB	Office of Management and Budget			
PPIF	Public-Private Investment Fund			
PPIP	Public-Private Investment Program			
PRA	Principal Reduction Alternative			

Office of Financial Stability

Contact information:
Department of the Treasury – Office of Financial Stability
1500 Pennsylvania Avenue NW
Washington, DC 20220
Telephone 202-622-2000 - Treasury Press Office 202-622-2960

Websites:
www.FinancialStability.gov
www.MAKINGHOMEAFFORDABLE.gov

Documents Referenced in the AFR:

Monthly Reports to Congress
http://www.treasury.gov/initiatives/financial-stability/reports/Pages/Monthly-Report-to-Congress.aspx

The Financial Crisis Response in Charts – April 2012
http://www.treasury.gov/resource-center/data-chart-center/Documents/20120413_FinancialCrisisResponse.pdf.

Anniversary Reports
http://www.treasury.gov/initiatives/financial-stability/reports/Pages/TARP-Annual-Retrospectives.aspx

Agency Financial Reports, including 2013, 2012, 2011, 2010 and 2009:
http://www.treasury.gov/initiatives/financial-stability/reports/Pages/Annual-Agency-Financial-Reports.aspx

Housing Scorecard:
http://portal.hud.gov/hudportal/HUD?src=/initiatives/Housing_Scorecard

Making Home Affordable Monthly Reports:
http://www.treasury.gov/initiatives/financial-stability/reports/Pages/Making-Home-Affordable-Program-Performance-Report.aspx

www.financialstability.gov